Planetary Politics

Theory Redux series
Series editor: Laurent de Sutter

Mark Alizart, *Cryptocommunism*

Armen Avanessian, *Future Metaphysics*

Franco Berardi, *The Second Coming*

Alfie Bown, *The Playstation Dreamworld*

Laurent de Sutter, *Narcocapitalism*

Roberto Esposito, *Persons and Things*

Graham Harman, *Immaterialism*

Helen Hester, *Xenofeminism*

Srećko Horvat, *The Radicality of Love*

Lorenzo Marsili, *Planetary Politics*

Dominic Pettman, *Infinite Distraction*

Eloy Fernández Porta, *Nomography*

Nick Srnicek, *Platform Capitalism*

Planetary Politics
A Manifesto

Lorenzo Marsili

polity

First published in 2021 by Polity Press

Polity Press
65 Bridge Street
Cambridge CB2 1UR, UK

Polity Press
101 Station Landing
Suite 300
Medford, MA 02155, USA

ISBN-13: 978-1-5095-4476-9 (hardback)
ISBN-13: 978-1-5095-4477-6 (paperback)

A catalogue record for this book is available from the British Library.

Library of Congress Cataloging-in-Publication Data
Names: Marsili, Lorenzo, author.
Title: Planetary politics : a manifesto / Lorenzo Marsili.
Other titles: Tua patria è il mondo intero. English
Description: Cambridge, UK ; Medford, MA : Polity Press, 2021. | Series:
 Theory redux | Includes bibliographical references. | Summary: "A
 manifesto for a new planetary vision that can address the great
 challenges of our time"-- Provided by publisher.
Identifiers: LCCN 2020026068 (print) | LCCN 2020026069 (ebook) | ISBN
 9781509544769 (hardback) | ISBN 9781509544776 (paperback) | ISBN
 9781509544783 (epub)
Subjects: LCSH: Political science. | World politics--20th century. | World
 politics--21st century.
Classification: LCC JA71 .M124513 2021 (print) | LCC JA71 (ebook) | DDC
 320--dc23
LC record available at https://lccn.loc.gov/2020026068
LC ebook record available at https://lccn.loc.gov/2020026069

Typeset in 12.5 on 15 pt Adobe Garamond
by Servis Filmsetting Ltd, Stockport, Cheshire
Printed and bound in Great Britain by CPI Group (UK) Ltd, Croydon

For further information on Polity, visit our website:
politybooks.com

Contents

Introduction   1

1 The twilight of universal Europe   5

2 The human zoo   21

3 The last ideology   35

4 Before the revolution   50

5 All under heaven   71

6 A glimpse into a politics for the planet   91

意味   129

Notes   133

Introduction

In 1972 Henry Kissinger met Zhou Enlai in what would become the first step towards the great reconciliation between the United States and China.

'How do you judge the French Revolution?' the American Secretary of State asked. 'It is still too early to tell', replied the Chinese premier. The scene has become a classic illustration of the Chinese inclination for the long term, despite probably originating in a misunderstanding in translation: Kissinger actually referred to the revolution of 1789, while Zhou Enlai thought of the French uprisings of 1968. Nevertheless, the exchange still gets it right. It is only today that the parable inaugurated by the French Revolution, with the entry of the nation as the leading historical actor and unique reference point for citizenship and political agency, finally comes to a close.

The Constituent Assembly elected during the French Revolution of 1789 drafted the 'Declaration of the Rights of Man and of the Citizen'. The title itself expresses the constitutive uncertainty of modern citizenship between the universal and the particular. In the Declaration we do not find a set of rights for all human beings and a set of rights reserved for citizens, but rather only those universal principles that unite the entire humanity. The universal aspect however goes hand-in-hand with the enshrining of particular rights in national law, which stands as their guarantee. The nation is both the guarantor of rights and the space for collective action by citizens to defend them. The nation, with its general will, is the instrument capable of establishing the universal in the particular and making the particular part of the universal.

We all know how much pain and destruction has emerged from such aspirations. The exclusionary character of the nation emerged immediately after the French Revolution, with the first great revolt in the French Caribbean led by the freed slave and black Jacobin Toussaint Louverture. Quoting the Declaration and singing the Marseillaise, Louverture found himself fighting that very same Republican army committed to extending across Europe new revolutionary principles that were apparently universal but actually denied to colonial peoples. We know the history of nations and we remember how often they turn against their own people in genocidal and persecutory acts. We know how arbitrary, and cruel, is often the choice of who really belongs to the nation.

But national aspirations fail today in another and deeper sense. The nation is no longer capable, even in its most ideal perspective, of guaranteeing human rights and the free exercise of popular sovereignty. Citizens' rights are no longer superimposed on, they are no longer the particular of, universal rights, but only a part or a subset of them. The nation, provincialised and marginalised, no longer guarantees full exercise of political, social and civic agency in a human society that has now trampled every border.

Many would like to convince us that the recovery of control and sovereignty passes by an abandonment of the world and an entrenchment behind the material and mental borders of closed territories and indomitable, great-again nations. But this idea has never been as false as it is today. If we do not want our political agency and our powers of the imagination to become a mere footnote in a tragic history of impotence, we must rather recover the planet and recuperate the belief in our power of transforming it.

In the pages that follow we will briefly run through the short history of the *becoming world of the world*, leading up to our contemporary sense of loss and disorientation. We will then offer some cursory notes for a possible planetary politics to liberate our world and our common humanity.

I

The twilight of universal Europe

The Avenida Central of Rio de Janeiro was built in 1904, following the latest European fashion: stone façades, domes and *belle époque* iron railings adorned a triumph of modernity. Photographers have left ample documentation of the elegant European architecture and of the people who frequented the street. Women are seen wearing outsized skirts and carrying black umbrellas, while men dress in dark tuxedos and top hats. We are at the equator: the temperature skyrockets and humidity causes the skin to sweat. These are not the right clothes to wear. But all climatic considerations are secondary, because *il faut être absolument moderne*. And being modern means disregarding distances, weather, and local customs, and thinking and acting as if we had all just left a café-concert on a Parisian boulevard.

It was in Brazil, in the hilltop village of Petrópolis, that Stefan Zweig took his own life in 1942. In his suicide note the great Austrian writer lamented the destruction of his 'spiritual home' – and, faced with the suicide of Europe, he committed his own. A continent in ruins lay on the other side of the ocean; a continent so dramatically different from the *belle époque* the planners of Avenida Central were out to imitate and so unlike that *universal Europe* that Zweig celebrated in 1916, in the middle of the First World War, with the following words of longing:

> Thus it grew, the new Tower of Babel, and never had its summit reached so high as in our epoch. Never had nations had such ease of access to the spirits of their neighbours, never had their knowledge been so intimately linked, never had commercial relations been so close in forming a formidable network and never had Europeans loved both their homeland and the rest of the world . . . The monument was growing, the whole of humanity counted

on assembling there for the consecration and music resounded around the edifice like a gathering storm.[1]

Here is all the inebriation of universalism that captured a European elite that had united the world in a single political, economic and cultural network. With a rhetoric that much recalls the apex of another and more recent phase of globalisation, the early twentieth century introduced the lexicon of the end of borders, of the overcoming of distances and of the political and economic interdependence of nations. Industry developed integrated supply chains on a global scale, trade and finance crossed every frontier, while telegraph lines, railways and steam ships connected the world, allowing the transmission of ideas, aspirations and fashions on a planetary scale as never before. Europe, with porous internal borders that could still be crossed without a passport, was swept by common political, artistic and cultural currents. The bourgeoisie of Buenos Aires adopted the latest Parisian *vogue* well before this reached the sleepy towns of the French countryside. And while four-fifths of the earth were under the control of a handful of Western powers, every corner of the world had its own Avenida Central.

Liberal capitalism and free trade embraced the globe, with an impenetrable and apparently indestructible web that gave rise to a thriving literature on European unity and world government. This was not, surely, a democratic and egalitarian universality. British supremacy stood as a guarantee of the stability of the system, a Janus-faced power that maintained order with the double gaze of its gunboats and its financial capital. A handful of European metropolises decided the fate of the world, while a large part of humanity experienced the squalor and crime of colonialism. The shadow of European domination and the global projection of its economy and trade transformed the life of every inhabitant, in every country, on every continent. From the Ottoman to the Persian Empire, from India to Japan, *the whole world* had to respond to and was transformed by the developments in one of its parts. It was something extraordinarily new.

Indeed, even in the colonised world, the other side of the coin of European sovereignty, a new feeling of transnational solidarity between oppressed peoples began to develop. When Japan annihilated the Russian fleet at Tsushima and defeated the Russian Empire in 1905 – marking the first victory of an Asian people against a European power – Turkish, Persian, Egyptian, Chinese and Vietnamese newspapers celebrated. Sixteen-year-old Jawaharlal Nehru, future Indian Prime Minister; Sun Yat-sen, the future leader of the Republic of China; Mustafa Kemal, who under the name Atatürk would become the father of modern Turkey; all cheered in unison. The Turkish writer Halide Edip named her son Tōgō in honour of the Japanese admiral who secured victory, while the future Indian Nobel laurate Rabindranāth Tagore improvised a triumphal march with his students in a small school of rural Bengal.[2]

The upheaval was total. 'A new model of life', wrote the economist Karl Polanyi, 'unfolds on the world with a universal aspiration without parallels from the time when Christianity began its history.'[3]

The mind in crisis

The carnage of the First World War destroyed the illusion of having rebuilt the universality that

Greek philosophy, Roman law and Christian religion had imprinted on the collective unconscious of European elites. The words with which Stefan Zweig continues his narration of the new Babel are those of a trauma: 'And it was precisely this generation of ours, who believed in the unity of Europe as if it were a Gospel', he writes, 'that was inflicted the annihilation of all hope, the experience of the greatest war among all the nations of Europe; our spiritual Rome was once again destroyed, our Tower of Babel once again abandoned by the builders.'

A feeling of loss, of disorientation and of inexplicable anger became a key element of the literature of the time. Here is how guests woke up in a morning of 1914 in a Swiss sanatorium; a place that, with its cosmopolitan diversity, its neuroses, and its privilege, provided the perfect representation of old Europe: 'What was this, then, that was in the air? A rising temper. Acute irritability. A nameless rancour. A universal tendency to envenomed exchange of words, to outbursts of rage – yes, even to fisticuffs. Embittered disputes, bouts of uncontrolled shrieking, by pairs and by groups, were of daily occurrence.'

Hysterica Passio is the title of the penultimate

chapter of Thomas Mann's masterpiece, *The Magic Mountain*. The next and necessarily last chapter is *The Thunderbolt*, referencing the shot that would bring all mountain guests back towards the valley, each behind his own border and with a bayonet at hand. Hannah Arendt, reflecting in 1951 on the consequences of the First World War, relied on almost identical words to Thomas Mann's narration:

> Nothing perhaps illustrates the general disintegration of political life better than this vague, pervasive hatred of everybody and everything, without a focus for its passionate attention, with nobody to make responsible for the state of affairs . . . It consequently turned in all directions, haphazardly and unpredictably, incapable of assuming an air of healthy indifference toward anything under the sun.[4]

They are words that sound a strident note of familiarity in today's Europe and indeed in today's world. With a continent and a planet once again torn by political conflict and dominated by divisions, hatred, and the spasmodic search for a scapegoat.

The fracture of 1914 and the collapse of *universal Europe* were experienced as a moment of great anguish and of psychological disorientation. Trauma touched everyone's life. Tens of millions of people found themselves without a homeland, expelled and rejected, in the first real crisis of refugees and stateless peoples of the modern era. But even those who still kept a place to call home felt the new division of the continent on their skin. Just think of *Jules and Jim*, the beautiful film by François Truffaut, where the playful pre-war *ménage à trois* is divided by a hard border, by mutual distrust and by the cruel looks that French and Germans exchange on the trains. It is not surprising that for the intellectual and economic elite the collapse of the Tower of Babel was perceived as an expulsion from Eden and as a crisis of European *civilisation*.

The words pronounced by Paul Valéry in 1919, in the aftermath of the armistice, are telling and well known: 'we, civilisations, now know ourselves mortal'. The feeling of a civilisational breakdown was well captured by the external gaze of Liang Qichao, one of the leading modern intellectuals of early twentieth-century China. In 1919 Liang found himself representing the new-born Republic of China at the Versailles peace conference; he travelled through a continent in rubble and noted his disillusionment with Western modernity. In his diary we find the following revealing encounter with an American journalist: 'And once back in China', the journalist asks Liang, 'will you take Western civilisation with you?' 'Sure!', Liang answers dutifully. 'Oh no!', the journalist replies, 'but Western civilisation is bankrupt!' Silence follows. 'And you', Liang finally dares to ask, 'once back in America, what will you do?' And the answer, which will profoundly influence the Chinese thinker, comes caustically: 'I will lock myself in my house and wait for you to bring Chinese civilisation.'

This 'crisis of the spirit' provided the focus for much of the writing of the period. But this was a crisis in bad conscience, a cultural and spiritual turmoil that actually represented the flip side of the structural crisis of European domination over the world. The crisis of civilisation of the 1920s stemmed largely from the *provincialisation* of Europe, from the diminishing economic and political role of the Old Continent at a time when the world was surpassing its old masters and beginning its path of emancipation. It was the emergence of a world beyond Europe that put Europe itself in crisis.

The First World War took away the universal system that hinged around the undisputed dominance of the British Empire. The central empires of Austria and Germany crumbled. France and Italy came out of the conflict traumatised. And following the gigantic butchery, Europe found its already feeble legitimacy all but dissipated: the civilising mission of the white man proved itself to everyone for the barbaric pillage it had always been. It is no coincidence that the first real public debate on the colonial situation began in those years, something that would soon lead to the emergence of the concept of 'decolonisation'. Economically, all European states emerged from the conflict heavily indebted to the United States: it was bankers in New York who now decided the destiny of the Imperial cabinet. The United States started casting its shadow over the world, strengthened by the moral legitimacy of the internationalist President Woodrow Wilson and by an economy that had surpassed that of the British Empire in influence and size. The world no longer looked to Parisian architecture but to the functionalist skyscrapers of the new American metropolises. It was perhaps Leon Trotsky who put it in the most explicit terms: Europe, he argued, found itself in the same position, vis-à-vis the United States, once occupied by the countries of South-Eastern Europe in relation to Paris and London. They had all the vestiges of sovereignty, but none of the substance.[5]

The crisis of European civilisation was nothing but the crisis of the sovereignty of the great European powers. Indeed, as paradoxical as it may sound, it was precisely the decline of European nation states that became the source of the great nationalist uprising that would lead the continent towards totalitarianism and a Second World War. This paradox is something that Hannah Arendt already identified in her famous study on the origins of totalitarianism. Like a weakened animal, scared and hence ready to bite, nationalism became the response of a body that had lost its vigour. Nationalism, then as now, is a response to a structural crisis of the national form. And if we dig deeper into the great resentment that characterised yesterday's as much as today's age of anger, what we will find is this: impotence.

The first *ouroboros*

Here is another paradox: the crisis of Eurocentric globalisation and of the unity of the world praised by Zweig manifested itself through the emergence of a world that became *increasingly integrated* and emancipated from its partial and provincial European origins. *More world* emerged from the crisis of the pretence that was European universalism.

The Babel that followed the end of *universal Europe* was very peculiar. If, on the one hand, the period between the two world wars certainly saw the impetuous growth of nationalism and protectionism, it is equally true that the causes of the multiple military, political and economic crises that would ultimately produce the fracture of the imperial and Eurocentric order all served to highlight and deepen, *through the unfolding of the crisis itself,* the extraordinary interdependence reached by the world system.

With a dialectical flip, the globalisation of railways and world markets took a leap forward and acquired greater self-consciousness precisely through the extraordinary novelty of its disintegration: a war that went from a skirmish on the border between Austria and Serbia to a conflict involving almost the whole of humanity; a Wall Street crash that brought the world financial system to its knees in a matter of days. Indeed, what is the purpose of the word 'great' prefixed to the war of 1914 and to the depression of 1929 if not to signal its unprecedented *planetary* character? Counterintuitively, it was the very existence of a deeply interconnected world that was revealed by the path of its implosion. And so the rupture of imperial globalisation was at once an unveiling and a deepening of the unity of the world.

Take a character such as Philip Raven, an economist in the service of the League of Nations and the protagonist of H. G. Wells's 1933 futuristic novel *The Shape of Things to Come*. Raven dreams of a world government and confesses that if it was the First World War that turned this idea into a working hypothesis, it was the Great Depression that led to the final realisation that human society had become one indivisible and integrated economic whole.

If the crumbling of European sovereignty, as Hannah Arendt recalled, leads to a hardening of totalitarian logic; if the new political impotence that Trotsky described leads to an increase in aggressiveness and to a recoiling on national identities; then it is always from this same contradiction that the theorisation of world unity, revealed and deployed through its crisis, takes a leap forward. Indeed, Wells's insights are not confined to the field of literature but accompany a new attempt to restore a political dimension to the system of global interdependence. The inter-war period was the backdrop to the first great proposals for the 'United States of Europe', from Jules Benda to Altiero Spinelli, and for a world order based on the League of Nations; it was precisely from this crisis that the search for the reorganisation of a new world system began. And it is in this context of unripe globalism that an ideology that would define the lives of billions of people decades later would also be born: neoliberalism. We will come back to this shortly.

We can perhaps think of the image of the *ouroboros*: the famous symbol of a snake biting its own tail and forming a circle that perpetually overcomes and renews itself. The implosion of *universal Europe* represented a turn of the screw, or better, a full circle of the *ouroboros*, which further tightened the universal character of the world, overtaking the limited remit of Europe itself. The *ouroboros* is the symbol of a process of *becoming-world of the world*, a process that deploys itself through the crisis of an order – the painful moment the snake reaches and bites its tail – that already contains within itself a further deepening of world interdependence, another round of the circle.

From a war that threw a world system to dust and yet prepared the cocoon for its over-coming emerged a planet that was increasingly intertwined and that towered over a weakened national politics. It was Antonio Gramsci who clearly identified the new playing field: 'The whole post-war period is crisis', he wrote, and 'one of the fundamental contradictions is this: that while economic life has internationalism or better cosmopolitanism as its necessary precondi-tion, the life of states has increasingly developed in the direction of nationalism.'[6] Or, in other words, the global deployment of economic forces tramples and overcomes weakened national polities.

The history of the twilight of *universal Europe* presents the opening sequence of the long crisis of the nation state. And if Gramsci's words appear to be written today, that is because it is at this historical juncture when first emerged the contradiction that now occupies the front pages of our newspapers.

2

The human zoo

Human zoos were one of the vilest colonial practices. Since the end of the nineteenth century they served to put conquered civilisations on display for the enjoyment of the curious crowds. The practice continued all the way to 1958, with the last organised on the occasion of the Brussels World Fair. There are still photos that bear witness to the horror. In one of them we see a woman stretching her arm through the fence and leaning towards a black child, offering her a banana. The woman is dressed according to the latest fashion of the *Glorious Thirties*, the thirty years of extraordinary economic acceleration that followed the end of the Second World War. She has perm in the hair, sunglasses, a bracelet on her wrist and a jacket with wide shoulder pads. She is a *Nouvelle Vague* posterchild, dressed as if she had just left a set of Jean-Luc Godard. And with all her fashionable modernity she leans towards the Other who is still less than human. We are at the heart of Europe and at the heart of the post-war economic boom. We are still in the heart of darkness.

When many today, with a feeling of unjustified nostalgia, are turning their gaze to those happy years, we must understand just how much the extraordinary acceleration in the West derived from an international agreement – from a new arrangement of the world that followed the fracture of *universal Europe* – and how privileged was our position within it.

Planning the world

The aspiration to rebuild a world through political and human rationality, mending the spiralling chaos of the 1920s and 1930s, was resumed in the last years of the Second World War. The blueprint for the peace that would follow began to be defined in the midst of the conflict. The Bretton Woods negotiations have thus become a key passage in the narrative on globalisation, becoming a mythical moment, in some ways a lost *el dorado*, in recent political thought. In 1944 hundreds of delegates from forty-four allied countries met in an obscure New Hampshire town with an ambitious goal: drafting the agreement that would regulate international trade and monetary policy for the capitalist world after the war. The nationalist hubris that followed the implosion of the imperial system made clear to everyone – and especially to the United States – that only a new political organisation of the world could prevent a repetition of the tensions that led the world to war.

The most celebrated recent example of state interventionism in a capitalist democracy was undoubtedly Roosevelt's New Deal. This was an ambitious economic transformation plan that, during the Great Depression, saved American capitalism from itself by transforming it. Through a mix of free market and socialism, the New Deal redefined the perimeter of state intervention in the economy, elaborated new redistributive structures, introduced elements of planning and dismantled the *laissez-faire* market absolutism characteristic of early liberalism. Inspired by the success of this initiative, the Bretton Woods conference tried to develop a new global agreement capable of combining free market and social welfare. This is how today's global infrastructure – now dramatically transformed by neoliberalism – first came about: the International Monetary Fund was meant to deal with payment and budget crises; the antecedent of the World Bank was tasked with promoting international development; and the GATT, the predecessor of the World Trade Organisation, was to organise trade relations between States through multilateral negotiation. In the same years, another international conference, in Dumbarton Oaks, was busy defining the role of the new United Nations, which was entrusted with the task of peacefully resolving disputes between states and developing elements of global coordination. This was the golden age of international planning.

Nevertheless, for a few decades the new structures seemed to hold up well, as international capital flows became regulated by state activism and the demands of free trade were counterbalanced by strong social and labour considerations. Nowadays, in the widespread feeling of economic and social crisis that characterises the West, the nostalgia for a return to that previous order is

omnipresent. Those were the years of the compromise between capital and labour, in which
capitalism seemed to be civilised and put at the
service of the many.

It is perhaps little known that the first debate
on the *end of ideologies* took place precisely at this
time, well before Francis Fukuyama introduced
the 'end of history'. In 1955 it was a Swedish
sociologist, Herbert Tingsten, who fired the
opening shot and described a politically pacified
world, where an unprecedented ideological consensus guaranteed a new compromise between
liberalism, conservatism and social democracy. In
France, in the same year, Raymond Aron echoed
him with almost identical words. While in the
United States the famous Harvard sociologist,
Daniel Bell, published a bestseller with a revealing title: *The End of Ideology: On the Exhaustion of
Political Ideas in the Fifties*. Such ideological lazi-
ness and drowsiness of conflict is the most evident
sign of an orderly and stable world organisation.

Paradoxically, it was precisely the *internationalist* construction of a new world order that allowed
greater freedom of action at national level. In
a clear rebuttal of those who today would like
to oppose national sovereignty and transnational

politics – portraying the struggle as one between patriots and globalists, or 'somewheres' and 'anywheres'[1] – it was precisely the political construction of an integrated world system governed by common rules that allowed the most extraordinary economic acceleration in history and gave a larger room for manoeuvre to national polities. The nation state was rescued by the internationalism of the architects of Bretton Woods.

The rest of the world

Such rosy vision of the post-war period is however highly partial and revealing of the blind spots of our privileged thinking. Western states were indeed taking off, but they were doing so in the wake of a world system cut to *their* interests. The very discourse on the end of politics inaugurated by Tingsten, Aron and Bell clearly marked the distinction between those who found themselves in a central and privileged position in that system and those who remained peripheral and subordinated. Ultimately, Bretton Woods and post-war social capitalism were based on colonial exploitation abroad and patriarchy at home. In those very years, in fact, the subalterns of the world rebelled against old and new imperialist oppression and women rebelled against the iron cage of the traditional family. It is no coincidence that nostalgia for that era is today mainly limited to certain categories of people in Western Europe and the United States: it is a model cut around the figure of the male, white and Western breadwinner. In fact, while in the West one could speak prematurely of the end of ideologies, the rest of the world was in turmoil. Frantz Fanon, one of the most important theorists of postcolonial thought, opened his seminal text *The Wretched of the Earth* in 1961 with words that were anything but post-ideological: 'Decolonisation, which sets out to change the order of the world, is, obviously, a programme of complete disorder.'

It is essential to recognise – and all the more so nowadays, with so many deluded by the dream of turning back the clocks – that the post-war system was heavily dependent on a global division of labour that saw a small percentage of the world's population prosper and a large majority survive in abject and persistent misery. As the North developed, the global periphery saw colonial extraction, long wars of independence and the occasional murder of leaders unpalatable to the West – as happened in 1961 to the Congolese leader Patrice Lumumba, assassinated with the connivance of the former colonial power (Belgium's official apology would only come in 2002). If it was a certain kind of global agreement that supported post-war social capitalism, then this agreement was built *by* and *for* Western powers. The human zoo, while disappearing from the public eye, remained internalised in economic and power relations. National sovereignty, partially restored to Western states by the international agreements of Bretton Woods, remained little more than a myth if one did not belong to the small group of highly industrialised countries.

It is precisely from the revolt against such conditions that the crisis of this model will emerge. And it will be, as with the crisis of *universal Europe*, the *nature* of its implosion that will turn the screw of world unity ever tighter.

Although the new order was imagined for the use and consumption of Western powers, the promise of a world based on the cooperation of independent states and orchestrated by the international institutions of Bretton Woods and the United Nations was taken seriously by many of the countries that were gaining their

independence from the old colonial masters –
more than fifty by the end of the 1960s. Since
its foundation, the United Nations General
Assembly had been trying to embody the spirit
of this new world order. While the Security
Council remained paralysed by Cold War divisions, the General Assembly often took the lead.
This is how it came to debate the fascist regime
of Franco in Spain, to carry out the partition of
Palestine, to manage former colonial territories
placed under its administration and to show a
particular intransigence towards the struggles for
national liberation in the Maghreb and Africa.
Nehru's India, for instance, successfully cam-
paigned against the segregation of the Indian
population in South Africa, with the newly independent Indian government managing to outvote
South Africa – and its British allies – to obtain an
official condemnation by the United Nations.

Transnational initiatives began to multiply in
an attempt to develop a tangible counter power
to Western domination. Among the best known
was certainly the Non-Aligned Movement,
which emerged in 1955 with a famous conference
in Bandung, Indonesia. But international struggles for decolonisation and economic justice were

widespread, and could be found, for instance, in the Tricontinental, with the first meeting in Cuba inflamed by the words of Frantz Fanon. In 1964 the G77 was born, bringing together a large number of developing countries around the demand for greater equity in the organisation of world trade and economic relations; in 1973, during the fourth meeting of the Non-Aligned Movement in Algiers, the idea of a new system of international relations was launched; the following year, during the General Assembly of the United Nations, the proposal for a 'New International Economic Order' (NIEO) was officially put forwards.

The NIEO advanced demands for a reconfiguration of the world that emerged from Bretton Woods, including redistributive justice, colonial reparations, sovereignty over natural resources, stabilisation of commodity prices and reform of multilateral organisations.[2] The United Nations Centre on Transnational Corporations would follow in 1974 to develop a blueprint of an international regulation, tackling issues such as the relationship between multinationals and national economic policy, the repatriation of profits, and technology transfer. These are the same issues that, unresolved, are still with us today: from the scandal of pharmaceutical patents to the transfer of profits to tax havens. With great foresight, and well before the digital revolution would make headlines, demands for global justice extended to the issue of information technologies. As NIEO was being advanced within the UN, the global South proposed a 'New International Information Order' to UNESCO, aiming to open up and democratise a communication system virtually monopolised by Western interests and companies. It is as if, today, countries united across the globe to open up a democratic alternative to the forced choice between Silicon Valley and Chinese technological infrastructure.

On the whole, the actions of the G77 mounted a challenge to reform the global institutions and the compartmentalised world organisation of the post-war period. The idea that development would be reached by mimicking the trajectory of industrialised nations was revealed as a lie: there was no linear trajectory leading from underdevelopment to development *within the same system,* since both poles were complementary, mutually dependent and defined by their position in the given international structure. That meant *there was no changing the country without changing the world*, making the overlap of internal and external, home and foreign policy evident to all. But now it was not up to the West but the rest to try and change the world. It was a frightening novelty.

'Ho Chi Minh, Mao Zedong'

The challenge posed to the West became compounded with two other simultaneous confrontations: one developing *between* the countries of the so-called First World themselves, and the other *within* each of those countries. On one hand, a clash developed between the United States and the industrial powers reborn through the post-war economic boom, with Japan and West Germany in the lead. Economic competition caused a growing American trade deficit, which would eventually lead the United States to decide to blow up the Bretton Woods agreements.[3] On the other, workers and students increasingly questioned the dominant economic model from the inside, through demands for wage increases, reduction of working hours, redistribution of wealth, workplace democracy and a reversal of hierarchical relations within industry and family. The late 1960s and the 1970s saw a well-known and extended season of protest that would lead many industrialists to question the resilience of the capitalist system in advanced democracies.

As European students took to the streets chanting 'Ho Chi Minh, Mao Zedong' the challenges linked and reinforced one another, bringing a double squeeze to post-war capitalism. Indeed, the most advanced sectors of the world's population could base their revolt precisely on the benefits of their privileged position in the world system – because the demand for wage increases is all the more irresistible the higher is the employment rate – while a revolt by the postcolonial peoples demanded a fair right of participation in Western economic surplus.

This is how support for the idea of a world order planned and agreed through international political cooperation slowly began to fade away. Too much democracy in the system risked jeopardising acquired privileges – between states as much as within them. The Western system was in crisis and the world at a crossroads: either overcome the international model of Bretton Woods accepting the demands of 'the rest' through a real democratic globalisation or find a solution capable of sublimating the demands coming from the Third World and from Western workers.

It was, once again, the *partiality* of the really existing world organisation that was being challenged. Just as *universal Europe* found its terminal crisis in the loss of its global domination and in the emergence of the rest of the world, so the post-war human zoo found its crisis in the contestation and deconstruction of a model built by and for a small group of Western countries. The crisis, once again, brought out *more world* through another turn of our *ouroboros*, a further tightening of the screw of world unity.

What was to be done? Internationally, colonialism was definitely out of fashion. Internally, repression of protests and the coercion of workers were locking industrial countries into continuous and widespread social conflict. A magical solution was found. One that would give yet another push to the becoming-world of the world and usher in a new global order: ours. The one that we see dying in front of our eyes.

3

The last ideology

China / Avant-Garde was the first public exhibition of contemporary art in Chinese history. In February 1989, at the end of a decade marked by tumultuous growth and new cultural ferment, a giant black sheet was laid on the steps of the National Museum of Fine Arts reading *No U-Turn*. The atmosphere was tense, the disorientation palpable: it was the first time most visitors had come into contact with a shamelessly contemporary artform. One performance above all turned out to be tragically prophetic: artist Xiao Lu drew out a gun and shot at her own work. It was something unacceptable to the authorities. The police stormed the museum and the exhibition was immediately shut down. Just four months later machine guns would resonate across Tiananmen Square.

The massacre that followed would shatter the dreams of a generation. The West began to realise that liberal democracy did not have to be the natural evolution of economic growth. On the contrary, if the repression made a part of Chinese society despaired and despondent, the path of reform did not stop, but accelerated. The demand for greater freedom was not merely disregarded and repressed but rather sublimated and transferred from the political to the economic level. In 1992 President Deng Xiaoping embarked on a Southern tour where he pronounced words that would remain famous: 'getting rich is glorious'. This was the real gunshot that would propel China forwards in the race of globalisation.

As often the case in times of crisis, the years marked by the fracture of the post-war order were fertile in debate and intellectual research – in China, where the term *Culture Fever* was coined to describe the ferment of the 1980s, as in the West. If the crisis following the First World War was understood as a crisis of civilisation, the waning of the Bretton Woods international system promoted a revival of that line of enquiry and was openly interpreted as a crisis of *modernity*.

Postmodernism, making its way through the 1970s and 1980s, condemned and renounced the binary thought at the basis of the apparatus of Western exploitation, of the global division of labour, and of the hierarchical, traditional and patriarchal order of societies. The relationship between self and other, between centre and periphery, that is, the relationship between coloniser and colonised, between industrial and agricultural states, between authority and obedience, was made to implode through the celebration and liberation of difference. The approach was liberating: it untied all identitarian rigidities and brought human freedom into play. It was desecratory: it tried to dissolve the most long-standing power structures, and among them patriarchy, the nation state, and the dialectics of colonialism. And it was cognitive: it introduced the new subjectivities of immaterial labour that were no longer represented by traditional industrial capitalism based on factory shifts and assembly lines. The post-war system was suddenly cast as unfair, extraordinarily old, and terribly boring.

But while postmodernism unleashed the energies of difference in open defiance of the domination of capital and of colonial states, capitalism and the very logic of domination morphed. They began themselves to abandon rigidity and dichotomous divisions and started to capture the same fragmented and dynamic logic at the base of postmodern thought, reformulating the distinction between centre and periphery and the boundaries of privilege and exploitation. Just as in the case of Deng Xiaoping, the demand for greater freedom was sublimated from the political to the economic level and put to use in the reorganisation of a world in crisis. Neoliberalism – the last of modern political ideologies – entered the scene.

Neoliberalism reorganised Western cognitive space. Like liberalism with imperialism first, and the post-war social market economy with the Bretton Woods institutions later, neoliberalism emerged through a reorganisation of the world system and inaugurated a further cycle of our *ouroboros*. But where *universal Europe* was built and maintained by imperial states, and while the Bretton Woods system was negotiated and agreed by nation states within a political and multilateral framework, the neoliberal system introduced the deliberate use of the market as an instrument capable of creating and maintaining a world economic order based *on the absence* of a political order of the same level.

The theory of two worlds

Let us return briefly to where we started. The predicament of one country above all represented the new Babel of nationalities, borders and mutual distrust that followed the First World War: Austria-Hungary. The multinational empire saw its territory drastically reduced and divided into a myriad of newly independent nations; a single economic space became divided into several protectionist and competing national economies. If there was one country that represented the fragmentation of the old imperial order and the collapse of European universalism this was it. It is not surprising that a young Austrian economist, Friedrich von Hayek, was inspired precisely by the peculiarities of that experience to develop an intuition that would change the world.

In 1978, looking back at his time as a soldier in the Austrian army during the First World War,

Hayek recalled how in the last days of the war he began thinking of the possibility of a 'a double government', and namely 'an economic government and a political government'. It is in the days of the defeat of Austrian imperial power that Hayek wonders whether it is possible 'to separate the two things – let the nationalities have their own cultural arrangements and yet let the central government provide the framework of a common economic system'.[1]

The model of the 'two governments' gained in urgency with the collapse of *universal Europe*. How could economic universalism be protected without relying any longer on British gunboats? The answer was a sophisticated theory that half a century later would become the ideal instrument to discipline rebellious colonial subjects and unruly Western workers. Hayek's Austrian intuition would be developed and used to separate, on the one hand, the multiple national sovereignties acting politically within state borders, and, on the other, a single imperial (*global* would become the favourite word) economic space anchored on an international web of trade, financial and economic *conventions* capable of limiting the space for manoeuvre of national sovereignties.

Carl Schmitt would describe this division by appealing to Roman history, and notably to the distinction between *imperium* and *dominium*. Imperium refers to the exercise of statehood: national laws, administration and the monopoly of violence. It is a world of nation states, each with its own prerogatives and sovereignty. While *dominium* refers to the world of *things*, and especially *money*. It is a world that exercises its power and follows its own rules independently of the first. Hayek, for his part, would refer to two distinct Greek terms to define the different exercise of power in each of the two worlds: *taxis*, identifying the strictly political and intentional organisation, and *kosmos*, defining the spontaneous order that the market should represent (but which, in reality, needs continuous codification and connivance by states and national elites).

The conceptual distinction between the external and the internal – between what lies outside and inside the border – is now fully trampled over. The two worlds intertwine and collapse into each other, as each human action comes to inhabit both simultaneously. The world of the *dominium* of money limits the world of the *imperium* of national laws and power, just as the latter hinders or facilitates the former. Schmitt, a passionate advocate of national sovereignty, to such an extent that he would be led to support the Nazi regime, stigmatised this division as causing a restriction of political agency. Neoliberal thought, on the other hand, saw it as the best representation of its own worldview.

It is so that the sovereignty of imperial gunboats is replaced by a global web of overlapping and intertwined legal and institutional conventions, laws and treaties that overcome and limit the space of manoeuvre of any state. While financial blackmail replaces – in part – the coercive power of military intervention. It is precisely this web, this *government of conventions,* that forms the new Leviathan that comes to guarantee the unity of the world system.

Discipline and punish

We are now in a position to understand why neoliberalism, first theorised in the aftermath of the First World War, was rediscovered at another time of crisis of the world system. Not so much, this time, because there was a risk of a return of nationalism. But, on the contrary, because of the approaching threat of a *political* world negotiated on an increasingly egalitarian basis. And where the supranational structures that emerged in the post-war period, beginning with the United Nations, risked becoming the Trojan horse for a democratisation of the world economic system and for an empowerment of the subalterns, the neoliberal idea of an international organisation *beyond* the reach of politics came back into the limelight. Rather than trying to define a new global arrangement through discussions, negotiations or concerted action – a highly risky operation, given the demands of former colonial states and the internal disagreement in the advanced world – the task of creating a new order was handed over to the market. Where military intervention and especially territorial occupation were becoming increasingly expensive and risky, neoliberalism offered a solution: market discipline.

It is precisely during this period that the institutions of Bretton Woods – starting from the International Monetary Fund and the World Bank – became highly charged instruments of international intervention. So-called structural adjustment programmes afflicted developing countries and tested the new neoliberal toolkit on governments that were too weak to choose otherwise. As African and Asian nations gained independence, they soon discovered that the Ministry of Finance remained occupied. Markets were opened wide, state property privatised and rights to exploit natural resources and land put up for sale, in a series of measures guaranteeing the continued extraction of value from the Third World. This marked the spectacular entry of what will be called *globalisation*.

States began to be placed in competition with each other to obtain the approval of international capital, or what Hayek's great American disciple, Milton Friedman, would call *the electronic herd,* which crosses the planetary steppes looking for the greenest grass. Attracting this flock would become the task of each state, and to do so they will have to wear what Friedman, who was never poor in captivating images, called the *golden straitjacket,* which meant empowering the private sector and reducing the role of the state, ensuring low inflation and prudent budgets, removing tariffs and restrictions on capital flows, privatising public industries, deregulating finance, and opening up basic services such as utilities, transport, and water to competition. International capital exploited the fractures created by the collapse of the Bretton Woods system to apply a market logic to international relations where the primary objective of each country, region and city was to appear attractive in a global competition for investment, and where the winning combination tended to be lower wages, tax breaks and minimum contractual and environmental protection.

Where the Bretton Woods system required a tortuous political struggle with the developing world and with the national electorate, neoliberalism was allowed to hide behind the supposed automaticity of the markets and of their mechanical herds. When, in 1997, the Malaysian Prime Minister complained of Western responsibility for the Asian financial crisis, Milton Friedman imagined the following response: 'There is just one global market today, and the only way you can grow at the speed your people want to grow is by tapping into the global stock and bond markets, by seeking out multinationals to invest in your country and by selling in the global trading system what your factories produce. And the most basic truth about globalization is this: *no one is in charge*.'[2]

What is most interesting is the expression in italics: *no one is in charge*. Is that really so? Friedman himself oscillates on this point, as he often speaks of the need for the US to maintain the integrity of the global system just as the British Empire did a century earlier. And so? What does this swing tell us? Is it just an instance of bad conscience, a desire to hide who is really in charge? Or is this the transformation of power into a spectre, such as to turn all dreams of insurrection into fancy? Perhaps both and more: because if, on the one hand, it is certainly true that the USA plays a preponderant and extraordinarily privileged role within globalisation, on the other, unlike the times of the British Empire, the system can now survive without leadership and even turn against those in command.

The rhizome

With much postmodern *jouissance*, the neoliberal dynamic dismembers the state and scatters its components on a planetary scale. Here lies the extraordinary novelty of this new turn in world unity and its moral coverage in terms of theory of justice. The dichotomy between inside and outside, between First and Third World, between centre and periphery, all become subjected to the refraction of a prism that diffuses development and underdevelopment, wealth and poverty, at the four corners of the globe.

The deployment of globalisation results in a deepening of the gap in class unity between a global elite and a nationalised citizenship. Reflecting the fragmentation of the world system, the rhizomatic recomposition of wealth and poverty leads to a similar reconstitution of the difference between classes. There is now more similarity in life habits, more community of interest – more 'imagined community', more nation! – between two professionals from London and Johannesburg than there is between them and the more peripheral areas of their own country. And while the elites are getting ever closer in a single global spider web, workers around the world are being pitted against other workers in an effective strategy of divide and rule.

Neoliberalism re-proposes the split between centre and periphery more and more *within* each community and less and less in the relationship *between* national spaces. This is the basis of the apparent paradox – which often informs many empty polemics between defenders and critics of neoliberalism – of a decrease in inequalities between countries and their increase within each state. We are witnessing a *zoning* of the world, with bands of privilege and exclusion living side by side.

From *Blade Runner* onwards, science fiction has shown us great metropolises where *the whole world* is enclosed within a city, with separate zones that appear like parallel universes and inhabit distinct temporalities. It is something we shy away from and prefer not to see. But it's here, all around us, right now. It's in Chicago, where the difference in life expectancy between the richest and poorest neighbourhood is an unbelievable thirty years, a gap greater than that between the United States as a whole and any other country. It's in Lesbos, beautiful Mediterranean island and open-air concentration camp for migrants. It's in the stations and ports of our great cities, places of segregation and daily violence that coexist with boutiques, shopping malls and high-speed travel. This is a process that we could call the self-colonisation of the world: the fragmentation of the globe into overlapping zones of privilege and exploitation living side by side.

The *rhizome* is a term borrowed by Gilles

Deleuze and Félix Guattari from botanical science. It indicates the peculiar growth of some plants that bring out bushes over an extended area giving the impression of separate plants emerging, whereas they are actually one entity connected by long underground roots. In a similar way, the new planetary extension of wealth and misery digs beneath every national frontier and connects social classes and interests, transforming external into internal differences.

The planetary deployment of neoliberalism, freed from the straitjacket of state control, stirs up power relations and throws up new and complex ethical problems. It cannot be right or moral for us to demand an impossible return to the previous capitalist system, the system that revolved around a relationship of dependence between centre and periphery and where the contentment of the West depended on the deprivation of the rest. The only moral alternative is to be found in an overcoming of neoliberal globalisation and in guiding a further turn of the screw, a further round of our *ouroboros*, towards a progressive planetary politics.

To do that, the time has come to understand what is happening all around us, right now.

4

Before the revolution

The rhizomatic deployment of globalisation lies at the root of the multiple crises that hit Western societies with the onset of the twenty-first century. As the control exercised by the Western core over the structures of neoliberal globalisation begins to be shaken off, the affluent, former 'centre' begins to tremble. And as a complex of economic, technological, migratory and ecological challenges that no state can match and govern come our way, the old inter-*national* system begins to shake.

We are all aware just how much the world's centre of gravity is shifting. We know that within a few years no European economy will qualify for the G8. We know that artificial intelligence, the real steam of the twenty-first century, sees a new cold war unfolding between the United States and China that entirely cuts off the old continent. We know that demography, which for many centuries has favoured a small Asian peninsula called Europe – a peninsula that has filled the world with its people as migrants, settlers and invaders – has now drastically reversed.

This horizontal provincialisation – the shifting of the world's centre of gravity – is accompanied by a second, vertical, and much more important shift. It is the provincialisation of our political and cultural forms in the face of the planetary challenges facing humanity. It is in fact the very idea of national dominion and control over the unfolding of the world that is coming undone, as *any* national system, even the most powerful, proves unable to govern the new planetary interdependence achieved. The words Jean Paul Sartre pronounced in 1961 regarding Europe apply today to the world as such: 'What has happened? Simply that we were the subjects of history and now we are its objects.'

Following the same paradox embodied by the crisis of *universal Europe* in the 1920s, and then by the crisis of the post-war system in the 1970s, it is once again more world that emerges and catches us off guard, unveiling a system that has become more advanced than its own representation and organisation. The becoming-world of the world leaps forwards, leaving us breathless and at the chase. It's another round of *ouroboros*. And this time we all find ourselves between the tail and the mouth of the snake. A century of world crises has produced an ever-closer union between different national communities, so that the internal life of each state has become part of a chain of economic, political and historical interdependence. We live at the time of the definitive collapse of any distinction between external and internal, of foreign and home policy, as our lives and our politics transform into a moebius strip where the outside folds into the inside and vice versa.

We know that artificial intelligence transforms our production models and the distribution of wealth as much as it shapes human consciousness and perception. We are aware of the risk that uncontrolled automation will lead to a world of endemic under-employment or miserable minijobs that place humans at the service of machine learning, while the ownership of algorithms and robots concentrates wealth in fewer and fewer hands. Abandoning control over our digital transformation would be paramount to abandoning entire sectors of our minds, and not only of our economy, to the control of a handful of private companies capable of directing industrial production as much as common sense. Well before robots steal our jobs the big data of multinational corporations will guide our thoughts and choices. This is nothing less than a new, extraordinary power of planetary scale that is totally unconnected with our democratic national political structures.

We know that inequality is structural to an economic model that embraces the entire globe and is premised on big business and petty politics, providing heavens for multinationals, purgatory for a few and hell for everyone else. We experience on a daily basis the impact of an economic system where international capital flows condition and blackmail immobile states. We know that the system of tax havens, a cornerstone of the scandalous accumulation of wealth in the hands of the very few and of the plundering of public finances, is based on competition between countries and on the absence of common, transnational fiscal policies. We know that it is precisely such international competition that grounds the global race to the bottom between workers, leaving hundreds of millions of people, in rich and poor countries alike, as a devalued commodity in a rigged market. The truth is that both large corporations and finance and technology now deploy a capacity for planetary action that is much more advanced and innovative than the old international system. And it is precisely from this advantage, from this historical overcoming, that they derive their privilege and their supremacy.

We know that global epidemics and health threats know of no borders. Indeed, the coronavirus crisis that broke out across the planet at the beginning of 2020 has shown the dramatic impotence of hard borders in protecting any of us against the invisible spread of a disease. If anything, the emergency has unveiled in a most dramatic form the concept of planetary interdependence. We have always known that pollution created anywhere has effects everywhere. And we are now realising how the divergent hygienic, health and welfare conditions around the globe are a threat to all of us. The lack of state-of-the-art healthcare anywhere is a threat to health everywhere. Not only has the virus exposed how investment in welfare and in public services is now a matter of national security; it has unveiled how economic inequalities across the world and the gap in public services between the richer and poorer countries are just as much a threat to our own national security.

We know, finally, that the organisation and survival of the human community depends on our response to the climate crisis. It is clear that no nation state is able to meet and govern this challenge in isolation. But there is more. It is the inter-*national* system itself that is accelerating the path towards disaster. Not only are traditional governance structures based on agreements between sovereign states, each bringing to the table its own short-term interests and jealousies, dramatically unable to face a global challenge of this magnitude. But, more importantly, it is precisely the system of nation states that perpetuates a competitive pursuit of wealth and power that renders our societies unable to overcome their dependence on the destruction of the planet. In a series of lectures on nationalism held at the beginning of the twentieth century, the Indian poet and Nobel Prize laureate Rabindranāth

Tagore stigmatised nations for blindly pursuing an increase in power and behaving like predators in an international jungle where the strongest survive and the weakest are devoured. Such increase in power, particularly today, is defined as economic growth. And international competition continues to drive states in a deadly race of hyper-production and hyper-consumption.

Simone Weil, writing in the 1930s, presented the problem explicitly with reference to socialist internationalism: 'Marx has shown well', wrote the French philosopher, 'that the real reason for the exploitation of workers does not consist in the desire to enjoy and consume of the capitalists, but in the need to enlarge the enterprise as much as possible in order to make it more powerful than its competitors.' The same applies to states, so that 'as long as there is, on the surface of the earth, a struggle for power, and as long as the decisive factor of victory is industrial production, the workers will be exploited'.[1] And the planet extracted and devastated. From CO_2 emissions to international competition on artificial intelligence and its military uses, all the way to downward competition on financial deregulation or workers' rights: in each of these situations 'I can only stop if you stop as well.'

This is why re-nationalisation, and in particular the retreat into the narrow confines of small European states, is the best guarantee of continued political impotence. It is no coincidence that the new agreement on the horizon sees the most economically privileged sectors actively cooperating with the new strong men of nationalism. Just as industrial capital and liberal elites were quick to change flags and support fascism in the tumultuous years of the implosion of *universal Europe*, the emergence of contemporary nationalism is often the political arm of the crisis of neoliberalism. The 'strongmen' authoritarian figures that emerged in the first decade of the twenty-first century demonstrate the perfect contiguity of interests between a nationalist, reactionary and patriarchal approach and the undisputed domination of financial capital and the 'straitjacket' of the competition between states. The fault line between populists and establishment, between nationalists and globalists, between open and closed societies begins to lose its meaning. We could speak instead of a turning point from neo-liberalism to neo-*illiberalism*, where contempt for democratic rules and nativist delirium become the new tools through which to keep the privileges of the few intact. Keeping nations apart and in competition with one another is the shortest avenue to ensuring the continued domination of unaccountable international capital. Here is the tragic, ridiculous task of nationalism.

The entire world finds itself provincialised and loses its grip on reality. Seven billion human beings lose control over their future, divided into their impotent national communities and at the mercy of an extraordinary transformation that *none of us* any longer lead and govern. We inhabit a world that has become a colony of itself, a planet unable to choose autonomously and forced to follow events that emanate from an inexistent imperial centre. The revolt of our times, too hastily attributed to austerity policies or to a backlash against a multicultural society, represents instead a rejection of the new condition of impotence that is the result of a world that has surpassed its organisation in separate nation states.

It is significant that it is Europe, the continent historically marked by global ambition and a dynamic attitude towards history, that has most clearly lost faith in the ability of politics to transform and govern the world. The result of this provincialisation, far from the push towards global justice hoped for by postcolonial theory, is individualism, nationalism and a myth of exclusion passed off as taking back control. Yet this is a transformation of planetary scope that unfolds in unison at the four corners of the globe, galvanising Indian as much as Brazilian nationalism, strengthening the authoritarianism of Turkey as much as of China, stimulating the dreams of power of Russia as of the USA. Nationalism is today a planetary movement. With the same paradox that we saw narrated by Hannah Arendt, today's grotesque nationalist shadow is nothing but the most obvious manifestation of the twilight of the nation state: the small, fearful dog that barks. It is a twilight that brings with it powerful psychological and cultural consequences.

The government of our psychosis

Something at once sweet and dramatic, identical and opposite to the *hysteria* described by Thomas Mann, happens towards the end of *Orlando*, Virginia Woolf's famous novel in which a fantastic and immortal character continues to change sex throughout the centuries. Suddenly all of Orlando's friends start getting married. Parties become ever rarer, frenetic and libertine lifestyles become the exception. Friends stay at home, cuddled by the security of the family. Orlando wonders what is happening around her. Soon, the First World War breaks out.

Catastrophe begins to manifest itself in individual behaviour well before it becomes an explicit historical development. Today, that vague feeling of collapse that lingers in the air does not have the nuptial characteristics found in Orlando but those of the *Homo oeconomicus* who stocks on supplies before the disaster. Indeed, the popularity of stockpiling – whether because of Brexit or viral epidemics or any other excuse – is a telling sign of a society that no longer trusts itself, inhabited by solitary, fearful individuals, dedicated to the accumulation of property and wealth as the only tangible certainty in a system that no longer guarantees any. It is a virus that affects everyone, from ordinary people, who are offered the placebo of a false concept of national sovereignty behind which to entrench themselves, to the many rich people who pathologically accumulate fortunes in tax havens and build bunkers in New

Zealand (there is a real movement of billionaire 'survivalists').

It is in fact not only the excluded and the have-nots who feel a loss of grip on the future. A similar feeling pervades many of those who scrutinise the system from the top. In the summer of 2018 technology theorist Douglas Rushkoff was invited by a group of billionaires to discuss the future. To his surprise the conversation rapidly shifted to the best strategy for adapting to what the billionaires called 'the event' – an interruption of civil life due to an environmental catastrophe, mass migration or a breakdown of political order. One question above all occupied them for more than an hour: how to keep control of security forces after the event, given that money will have become insignificant? When Rushkoff tried to suggest that the deployment of technology and a different economic and social approach could avoid such catastrophe, and that his interlocutors should focus their energies and resources on just such a task, the answer was a courteous shrug of the shoulders. Rushkoff came out of the meeting with one certainty: some of the richest and most technologically advanced individuals on the planet feel deprived of any agency to shape events.[2] Those who should rule the world are trading leadership for dystopia. They understand perfectly well that the paradigm must change but they no longer believe this may happen without a great catastrophe.

Precarity, no longer a simple working condition, becomes a primary existential trait. The perception of a vague, indefinite, imminent disaster that no one will be able to cope with leads to a privatistic chase towards salvation and to the renunciation of any vision of collective emancipation. The model of 'strongmen' emerging in all parts of the world reflects the search for a muscle that protects at a time when institutions, procedures, and the rule of law appear increasingly fragile and incapable of guaranteeing anything of substance. Here is the resolution of the postmodern fracture: weak thought, so suitable for moments of calm and hegemony, and so unsuitable for moments of uncertainty and anguish, is overcome by a new *strong* thought embodied by the muscular and phallic decisionism of the leader who acts as a simulacrum of an absent power.

The category of the *wall* perhaps represents this dialectic between impotence and muscle better than any. Contemporary walls, as the American philosopher Wendy Brown points out, express the human desire for protection and containment in a world unable to guarantee them. And yet walls are dramatically ineffective to make such protection real. The threats we face are not even remotely touched by slabs of concrete and barbed wire. On the contrary: walls are precisely the confession of our impotence. 'Counterintuitively', writes Brown, 'it is the weakening of state sovereignty, and more precisely, the detachment of sovereignty from the nation state, that is generating much of the frenzy of nation state wall building today.'[3] Closed borders represent the death knell of national sovereignty.

But what are muscles and borders for, then? Just like nationalism emerges as a palliative to the crisis of the nation, they are cheap toys for a cowardly political class offering to the electorate the illusion of control in a play of shadows. It is so, step by step, that our politics loses grip on reality and becomes the government of a collective psychosis. A failed group therapy. Where, like children, we all shut our eyes, pretending to have become invisible.

The Last Man

Just at a time when ideas for a *new world*, remade and reconfigured, would seem to be urgently needed, our conceptual apparatus and our intellectual ambition, provincialised just as much as our states, appear tragically unfit for the task.

With the emergence of neoliberal hegemony came the second, and far more important, crisis of ideology, which renounced to the metaphysics of truth and the grand narratives of modernity. *The Postmodern Condition*, the seminal 1979 text by Jean-François Lyotard, introduced the disbelief in history, progress and the human capacity to create order that characterise the relativism that would accompany the deployment of globalisation. At the end of the 1980s, in his *The End of History and the Last Man*, Francis Fukuyama delineated the boundaries of a pacified world in which democracy and liberal capitalism had definitively won the global race, making all utopian ambitions and aspirations for systemic transformation suddenly obsolete. At the beginning of the 1990s the American philosopher Richard Rorty – with a smirk that reminds us of the historical weariness characteristic of the zenith of a civilisation – threw a romantic gaze towards the Third World, hoping that 'it' might still be able to theorise and realise that different future that wealthy and pacified America was no longer able to imagine.[4] It was the very possibility of an *otherwise* that was forgotten and denied. Indeed, this approach was soon to be fully realised by Western political classes, which rushed to erase any difference between right and left and began competing for who liberalised finance the fastest, who precarised labour most effectively, who privatised the larger number of services and industries and who extracted wealth most profitably from our planet. This was what Mark Fisher would call *capitalist realism*; the idea that there is no alternative to really existing capitalism. It is a powerful virus that colonised our imagination, turning us into the *last man* of Friedrich Nietzsche, who inhabits an era saturated with history in which humanity runs into the dangerous disposition of self-irony and cynicism. This is the condition that makes it impossible to imagine a destiny spelled out in any form but the present tense. And it marks the end of world-making and utopia, or the possibility of placing intellectual and political ambition at the level of the *totality* and of a collective transformation of humanity as such.

If we distance ourselves from this time and look at this era *with the eyes of the future* – and notably with the eyes of those who experienced its crisis and its denudement with the financial implosion of 2008, the political turmoil of the 2010s, and the great geopolitical realignment in store for the 2020s – then perhaps its partial, partisan and, ironically, *ideological* character may come to the fore. However convinced and convincing may have been the debate around the end of grand narratives, of truth, even of history, the minds of Western societies appeared to be captured by a collective hypnosis and a great intoxication of meaning. Grand narratives and large-scale narrations did not end; they became transfigured into a new, unfamiliar *and hence invisible* ideological patchwork, just as the extraordinary diversity of greens that compose the rainforest appears invisible to the eyes of the profane.

Think of the feeling of the *picturesque*. When we walk through a historical centre – a common experience and the incredible heritage of many European cities – we relive a history that presents itself to us with the aura of a fulfilled speech, an amalgam of closed meaning. The *past* appears to us as a *presence*. Quite the opposite is the experience of strolling through the streets of a bland neighbourhood that is contemporary to us, where we barely notice the buildings and architecture that we cross. The *present* appears as an *absence*. But every neighbourhood has been someone's present and all will sooner or later be someone else's past, making the transition from absence to presence – or, in other words, our collective capacity for awareness of the whole – a matter of passage of time. Something similar happens with systems of thought. The end of ideologies and grand narratives has been nothing but the hidden *present* of an extraordinary, powerful ideology that finally shows itself to us with all the ostentation of those who scrutinise something that is *past*.

The postmodern ideology of the last man, of the end of grand narratives and of ideology itself appears today as a historically situated system of thought that is the expression of a very peculiar phase of Western modernity. There is a very telling moment in the first film of *The Matrix*. When, on the roof of a skyscraper and with a gesture sweeping over the skyline of New York, Agent Smith confesses to Neo that the matrix has been designed to recreate 'the peak of your civilisation'. How come we are so casually sold the idea that *our present*, the present of any spectator watching the scene at the cinema in 1999, is as good as it is ever going to get? Here is the perfect image of what that ideology meant: the celebration and flattening of the present, the idea that no alternative to it is possible or indeed even desirable, so much so that if we had to decide what fictional world aliens would be feeding our brain it could not be anything else but *right now and right here*.

This is the ideological framework that peaked at the turn of the millennium and entered into crisis immediately after. In the 2000s a pacified history apparently stuck on *presentism* accelerated once again. So much so that none of the certainty of Agent Smith remains just twenty years later. But what happens with the crisis of the *last ideology*? When a body accustomed to detachment suddenly finds itself embraced and implicated, fear and disorientation dominate. The collapse of the world of the happy matrix leaves behind a nihilistic wake of impotence, abandonment and apocalyptic thought. The oblivion of an alternative to *this* ideology and the closure of an institutional

alternative to *this* politics lead directly to a disposition that sees the overcoming of a historical
phase as the end of history itself, albeit this time
not in the smug satisfaction of Fukuyama but in
the despondency of general collapse. Recent years
have witnessed a flourishing discourse in popular culture around the apocalypse: TV is awash
with dystopic dramas, from *Years and Years* to
3%; a plethora of books on climate catastrophe is
published monthly; and in France there is even a
new genre called *collapsologie,* with its think tanks
and cult authors. It is the vision of the inevitable
collapse of an order against which our individual
and collective action appears powerless.

This is where we are: the decline of the nation-
state system, and of the privileged position of the
West within it, concocts a global insurgency that
takes up authoritarian vestiges to pretend it is still
in control. It triggers a psychosis that leads to fear
and entrenchment. And it thrives on a reduced
intellectual ambition that can no longer conceive
a transformation of the world as such.

How do we get out of this? We may certainly
choose to be tempted by the vision of the apocalypse, imagining that only a great catastrophe,
and therefore a great catharsis, will be able to

complete the next turn of the screw and emancipate our world from its shackles. History teaches us this is often the case. But history also teaches us the incredible unpredictability of human agency. We no longer understand the world. But what if we can't see Ariadne's thread because we are the thread ourselves? It is time to open up to the idea of a renewed planetary politics.

5

All under heaven

Try asking yourself this question: how much of our political crisis and of our perception of loss of control derives from a tragically outdated concept of the world and from the privileged position that our nations once occupied within it?

Recent Italian thought has sharply described the crisis of modern politics and the newfound impotence of social conflict and parliamentary struggle. This is hardly a coincidence: the parable of Italian decadence is perhaps the most evident representation of the fall of political possibility throughout the West. From the extraordinary vitality of the long 1970s and the peculiarity of having the largest Communist party of the West, Italy found itself, already in the 1990s, with an imploded political field, an increasingly atomised and idiotic society following the arrival of Silvio Berlusconi, and a parliamentary system blindly chasing the new neoliberal consensus. What emerged was petty politics and a lack of real alternatives. Recriminations about the loss of 'the political' multiplied: this is the idea, dear to thinkers such as Massimo Cacciari, that the space of politics is increasingly reduced and devoured by the space of economics and technology. Such analysis, ultimately rooted in Carl Schmitt, captures the effects of neoliberal deployment the world over, and Italy is but the canary in the mine. But what happens if we try to dissociate *the political* from *the national* and broaden our temporal and spatial gaze?

If we look with the eyes of the future at the years of neoliberal hubris we can perhaps begin to free ourselves from the spell of the end of politics. If we look at this period from the perspective of its end, then perhaps, just as the idea of an end of history and ideology appeared as yet *another* ideology, so the depoliticisation of society may appear as a *political* movement of unprecedented force. The neoliberal parable has turned the world upside down. And it has done so in London as in New Delhi, in Washington as in Shanghai, transforming the ways of life of billions of people, subverting economic and geopolitical relations and changing at the root the functioning of Western democracies. In reality, every transformation of the world order is always already political, albeit undemocratic, in that it acts through human agency and social structures and profoundly reshapes the pillars of our communities and of international society, redefining the boundaries, the playing field and the oscillation allowed between parties, interests and ideological positions.

Certainly, neoliberal globalisation reduces the space granted to democracy and conflict to direct the organisation of society when compared to the amplitude of the oscillation allowed within the previous, post-war system. A world order was more permissive – at least, as we have seen, for a privileged part of the world – than the one that followed. But if it is precisely *the ordering of the world* that we place in our field of vision, we realise that in reality popular sovereignty has always been little more than a decoration. The traditional structures of participation and conflict had little to do with the imperial structuring of the planet;

little did they contribute to the *Glorious Thirties* of American and Western post-war hegemony (if anything, they manifested themselves more strongly during the crisis of this model, accelerating it); little did they have to do with the establishment of neoliberal globalisation, which was actually devised again them.

The time has come to overcome the mourning for the reduction of political agency in Western democracies and ask ourselves the following question instead: how can we grant democracy real power and grip on the reorganisation of the world? At a time of extraordinary transformation such as ours, the real political question lies entirely here.

It is understandable that a Western generation who has experienced the apparent political effectiveness of the post-war consensus and was then thrown into the impotence dictated by neoliberal globalisation would find itself disoriented and prey to a powerful sense of *loss*. And so perhaps we need to look beyond the West to recover a sense of possibility and to untie the ambition to act from the weight of individual biographies. The historical and experiential parable experienced by a Chinese observer, for instance, is starkly different. Starting from the darkest years of Maoism – those same 1960s and 1970s that marked the height of social conflict and political imagination in Europe – contemporary reality presents itself in its full transformative power. If the European trajectory starts from the privilege of the post-war period, with its partial political freedom, to find itself handcuffed by a globalisation that has overtaken and harnessed its creators, the Chinese parable starts from a famine that claims tens of millions of victims and arrives today at the challenge launched to American hegemony. Albeit in less extreme ways, such divergence in historical experience is familiar to much of the non-Western world.

Take a contemporary Chinese philosopher such as Zhao Tingyang. One of his best-known texts, *Tianxia*, published in China in 2016, is based on assumptions very similar to those that inform the thought of the decay of the political:

As globalisation deepens, we see that that the biggest beneficiary is not a particular state, but the new power structures that exist in reticular form. The world financial capital system, the new media system as well as other high-tech systems are currently the main beneficiaries of the world structure and have the hope of becoming the world's greatest powers. Although these systems are still partially retained by sovereign states today, if we consider their current functioning and future prospects they are bound to increase their power, weaving their spider web around the world and progressively controlling all the spaces of action and speech. Step by step, they take states hostage and manipulate them (and this in part already happens), gradually transforming governments into agents of the world system of capital and technology ... these are the new authoritarian powers in formation.[1]

Zhao describes the process of detachment of globalisation from the control of any state, that 'nobody is in charge' at once true and false. What follows from this process is the emergence of *a world that becomes independent of the world*; that is, a web of forces, structures and flows that lie beyond the control of any nationalised political power and constitute an integrated network of planetary reach. The *theory of the two worlds* at the basis of neoliberal thought jumps forwards and surpasses the economic sphere alone: it is entire fields of our imagination that are now taken out of our control.

> There is no America. There is no democracy. There is only IBM and ITT and AT&T and DuPont, Dow, Union Carbide, and Exxon. Those are the nations of the world today . . . The world is a collage of corporations, inexorably determined by the immutable by-laws of business.

The famous monologue from the film *Network* in 1976 reflected growing anxiety at the time that corporate power could eventually overturn democracy. Today, we are witnessing the birth of a new kind of planetary powers, boasting genuine state characteristics: global corporate nations that can extend their powers across the entire planet. They are increasingly able to mobilise their own 'citizens' to shift public policy. Uber has been rallying its users to fight against greater public regulation of its business model, while AirBnB has been leveraging the interests of its users to avoid greater fiscal scrutiny. They can play states one against the other to remove regulations and provide large tax breaks. And they can utilise the personal information of billions of people to sway public opinion effectively and manipulate political views and politicians.

But what is most interesting is the answer Zhao offers to this state of affairs. Far from any nostalgia and far from any invocation of national power – and if there is one nation potentially able to govern such new powers, that is China! – Zhao takes up a concept of Chinese political philosophy, that of *Tianxia*, in order to advance the need for a new planetary politics as a way out of this predicament.

The concept of *Tianxia* finds its origins in the Zhou dynasty, roughly contemporary to the Greece of Socrates and Plato. The Chinese world was then divided between different political communities in perpetual infighting. One of them, the State of Zhou, managed to bring all the other states into its orbit. But Zhou was neither the largest nor the most powerful state. Rather, it achieved hegemony through the attractiveness of its system, the good governance that characterises it and the resulting economic vitality. As a minor state it did not have the strength to conquer and subjugate the others openly. And so, its hegemony became manifested through a more remote and often indirect form of government, held together by the construction of a system of interdependence between the different communities. The state of Zhou became the guarantor, through a sort of *ante litteram* federation, of all those 'common goods' that necessarily required cooperation beyond the narrow borders of the national territory of each community: such as, for instance, works to control the great rivers of the Chinese plains. Having to govern a larger unit without being able to exercise direct political and military control over all its parts, the question of 'world government' emerged as the central theme of civil and political relations between the different communities of the (Chinese) known universe. With the concept of *Tianxia* – literally, 'all that is under heaven' – the Zhou dynasty weaved a sophisticated system that embraced national plurality within a single territorial, political and moral space.

This is what allows Zhao Tingyang to present *Tianxia* as a concept capable of 'transforming the inside into the outside' and of defining 'a world that possesses its own world-ness', that is, 'a becoming world of the world'.[2] In other words, the ability to understand *the world as such* as a political subject and a yardstick for one's own actions. Although the reference to 'heaven' may suggest a religious idea, this is not the metaphysical and transcendental conception given to the word by the Christian faith. Chinese thought has never long entertained the hard division between being and becoming, between transcendence and immanence proper to Greek philosophy and Christian theology. *Tianxia*, 'all under heaven', rather refers to three exquisitely immanent dimensions.

The first is the *territorial* dimension. That is, the idea of taking the entire extension of the world as a point of reference for action and thought. It is precisely this dimension that we have seen becoming increasingly central in the rounds of *ouroboros* we described. Whether through the imperial extension of *universal Europe*, the postwar world planning or the universal *dominium* of neoliberal conventions, our recent experience has increasingly moved towards the inclusion of the world as a whole as a reference unit of our lives and communities.

The second is the *political* dimension. The presence of a harmonious order between 'all under heaven' is identified as a condition and guarantee for the well-being of any part of it. This is how the *Tianxia* world system transforms 'the world as such' into a political unity whose effects and functioning are fully interlinked, so much so that *governing the world becomes the premise for governing the country*. This is an extraordinarily modern conception of interdependence, finding in the correct functioning of a world system the prerequisite for the correct functioning of its individual components. Or, as we have seen in the case of the actions of developing countries united in the G77, the transformation of a world system is the necessary premise for the transformation of national life. To understand just how far our politics is today from this principle, one need only think of the reality of the European Union: where there was little scruple to sacrifice *a part of* the Union – and namely Greece in 2015 – for the maintenance of particular economic interests. Only then to realise, in retrospect, the chaos that would result and how such chaos would turn against all parts of the whole. From the clampdown on Greek demands for economic justice to the explosion of nationalism and Brexit the line is straight: because governing Europe has now become the premise for governing any single European country.

Well beyond Europe, as we have seen, the central tenant of neoliberal globalisation is precisely the construction of a homogeneous planetary economic space deprived of any matching political power. Blocking the emergence of a new 'supranational sovereignty' was always one of the precepts of neoliberal thought. Wilhelm Röpke, one of the most influential theoreticians of the new economic course, put it explicitly in 1955: 'Reducing national sovereignty is one of the most urgent needs of our time', but, beware, 'excess sovereignty should be abolished and not transferred to a higher political unit'.[3] This is a theme dear to much of the neoliberal tradition: globalism in the economy must never translate into a transnational democracy able to yield political power at that same level. It is when the ordering of the world ceases to be a space for organised political struggle that the premises of neoliberalism are realised.

The third and final is the *social* dimension. This is something akin to the *general will* of the world, or what, as the French say, 'tout le monde' desires. Governing *Tianxia* therefore means having the support of all the inhabitants of the world and not privileging one part over another.

Putting aside long discussions on the concept of the general will, the extraordinary modernity of this idea is to be found on a moral plane: it aims to take *the totality of humanity* as a point of reference to assess the desirability and legitimacy of an action *even if undertaken only by a part of it*. As we have widely seen so far, every round of globalisation in the recent past has dramatically failed this condition, positioning itself always on the side of someone and against someone else. The neoliberal system is actually based on the subversion of this principle, whereby the global integration of the productive system is premised on a process of social dumping and competition between states that unloads onto the weakest the weight of economic and wage competition.

Tianxia is therefore a concept of the world that unites its territorial extension (the total perimeter of sovereignty), its political structure (both in the directly planetary dimension of the exercise of politics and in the governance of interdependence) and its moral and social compass (taking as a reference the common welfare of all humanity). It is the union of all this that Zhao Tingyang calls 'the sovereignty of the world'.

This is the answer we can bring to those who

abandon themselves to the sorrow of a world in which our politics and our citizenship, in which our ambitions, aspirations and hopes, seem unable to shape the becoming of reality around us: if we believe our politics is in crisis, that is because our imagination has stopped at the borders of the nation state and at a conception of the world that has now been surpassed by the very evolution of the world itself. We must put aside the mourning and imagine a new way of governing and influencing the extraordinary planetary interdependence we have achieved.

A trace

Nation-building, in the reading given by the Italian Marxist and anti-fascist Antonio Gramsci, follows a double movement: on the one hand, the territory widens until it becomes that of the entire nation (and no longer, for instance, that of the medieval commune); on the other, the cosmopolitan element of Roman-Imperial and Christian culture shrinks, until it becomes nationalised and popularised. Intellectuals and elites develop ever closer ties within the new national community, a delimited territory wider than the medieval fief but more limited than the cosmos. The broadening of the territorial dimension of political authority and the diminishing of the universal horizon of belonging contribute to the formation of the nation state, sealing a new alliance between elites and people: a community of shared destiny.

This is precisely the mechanism that today breaks down and goes into reverse: a crisis that Gramsci had anticipated. In the last years of his life he began to identify a new political constellation no longer based on the territorial extension of the modern state but, rather, on industrialism and the boundless expansion of American capitalism. It is such economic power, untied from all territorial delimitation, that began to exceed and surpass the reach of the European states weakened and provincialised by the First World War. The outcome of this process was a new disconnection between elites and nation states. And where it was the nationalisation of the elites that gave life to the modern state form, then their denationalisation could only have a devastating effect: 'Already today', Gramsci wrote in the mid 1930s:

[A] phenomenon similar to that of the Medieval separation between the 'spiritual' and 'temporal' dimensions occurs in the modern world [. . .] traditional intellectuals, detaching themselves from the social grouping to which they had so far given the highest and most comprehensive form and therefore the widest and most perfect conscience of the modern state, perform an act of incalculable historical significance: they mark and sanction the crisis of the state in its decisive form.[4]

It is from here that Gramsci began to muse about the possibility of constructing a new political subject that would be no longer national but 'cosmopolitical', that is, capable of matching the planetary scale of the economic interdependency he saw building up around him. This is a very profound and, in some ways, extraordinary reversal of perspective. Gramsci had long stigmatised the cosmopolitan character of the Italian intellectual classes. He accused Italian elites of having been mesmerised by the memory of Roman imperialism and Christian universalism so as to have become unable to usher in a process of national construction at the same time as their European peers. This is what explained the backward condition of the Italian nation. But if this analysis is often used to turn Gramsci into a theorist of the centrality of national politics, his insights into the unfolding of a new supranational economic power would lead him wonderfully to rehabilitate the exceptionality at the basis of Italian backwardness. He wrote:

> The Italian people are the people who 'nationally' are more interested in a modern form of cosmopolitanism, collaborating to rebuild the world in a unified way is in the tradition of the Italian people, of Italian history [. . .]. The 'mission' of the Italian people is in the recovery of Roman and medieval cosmopolitanism, but in its most modern and advanced form.[5]

True, Gramsci now seems to be telling us, the commitment to cosmopolitanism characteristic of the Italians caused them to delay the construction of a modern nation state and weaken the country vis-à-vis their European peers; but at a time when the national construction begins to be overcome by new planetary economic forces, precisely that original sin could represent no longer an element of backwardness but a vanguard, facilitating the emergence of a cosmopolitanism for a new era.

What is a cosmopolitanism for a new era? It is *not* merely ushering in a new international organisation for our world – say, 'a new Bretton Woods', as is often demanded. Rather, it involves inventing political and cultural forms at an immediately planetary scale that are capable of living up to a world that has already surpassed its organisation and structuring through the relations between states. This means transitioning from an inter-*national* to a planetary political vision.

Italian nineteenth-century revolutionary Giuseppe Mazzini has provided one of the most telling descriptions of international progressivism, envisaging a world where independent nations acted on the stage as 'the individuals of humanity'. The image is that of a matryoshka: just as citizens relate to each other within a nation, so nations relate to each other within the world. The Italian republican hoped that such nations, freed from monarchical oppression, would give rise to a 'republic of nations' fostering the collective common good. Mazzini was never lacking in initiative, establishing a short-lived proto federation called 'The Young Europe'.

But such progressive internationalism leaves us right at the heart of the problem, amid the conflict and competition between states and between peoples.

On the one hand, and contrary to Mazzini's hopes, his logic provides today the backdrop to the depoliticisation of international relations generated by neoliberal globalisation. It is precisely this matryoshka-world that is overtaken by the neoliberal turn and by the creation of the new 'authoritarian powers' mentioned by Zhao Tingyang. Nations are pitted one against the another to limit the exercise of political agency at planetary level – or, in neoliberal parlance, to block the reconstruction of sovereignty at the level of the *dominium* of capital. So that we find ourselves today within a grotesque cosmopolitanism reduced to mere *cosmos* and in which there is no *polis*. On the other hand, such inter-*national* vision falls prey to the traditional dynamic of great power competition and to the blind spot isolated by Simone Weil – *I can only stop if you stop*.

Gramsci's cosmopolitical vision is alternative to Mazzini's internationalism in that it entails the development of new social, political and cultural practices of a directly planetary scale. It is not about federating nations or sitting national elites in joint summits to reach inter-*national* decisions, but rather organising citizens themselves and empowering them to act at the scale of the problem itself – without delegation via their nations. The European Union provides a good example of the distinction: the European Council, where heads of member states regularly sit together and negotiate common policies – with each protecting their interests and sovereignty – is the most advanced instance of inter-*nationalism* today. The feeble structures of European democracy – such as the European Parliament and the embryonic system of European parties – represent instead the first vestiges of the kind of transnational democracy that must inform a new planetary politics, whereby citizens organise together over and beyond their national borders and representatives. It is time to see what shape that may take.

6

A glimpse into a politics for the planet

The first two decades of the twenty-first century have been marked by a rapid succession of economic and political crises of planetary scale. We need to scale up our own practices, theories, and political and cultural conceptions for a world that has already surpassed our national and bordered thinking. What follows is a short set of notes for a possible direction forward.

Planetary parties

In November 2017, theatre director Milo Rau organised a general assembly in the German Parliament to which he invited representatives of civil society and political movements from all over the world. The idea was simple: German politics has an impact on the whole world, but the world has no say in it. This points to a more general characteristic of our political systems: our spaces of democratic participation, and notably political parties, operate within the borders of our nations, and this, familiar as it might appear, has at least two important shortcomings. The first, which Milo Rau's project directly related to, is the lack of any structure where *the rest of the world* can take part in those aspects of national decision making with the highest impact on the chain of global interdependencies. The second, instead, impacts national citizens directly: for so long as our political parties only act *within* the confines of our national parliaments and govern-ments, they shut themselves, and ourselves, out of any significant influence in shaping the direction of all that eludes national politics: and that means today's most important threats, opportunities, and challenges. The time has come to build those planetary political forces which, almost a century ago, at the dawn of the modern caesura between the nation state and the unfolding of the world, Antonio Gramsci imagined.

In 1989 the first congress of the *Transnational*

Radical Party was organised in Budapest, starting from an idea of a small group of Italian activists, intellectuals and radical MPs. The ceremony sanctioned the realisation of the intuition, insane for the time and bordering on agitprop, to build a genuine transnational party in the waning years of the Cold War. While the Berlin Wall was about to collapse, a dense network of radical activists tried to weave a web of political participation on a transnational scale. Representatives of the party were sent to Yugoslavia, where, despite collecting various expulsion orders, they obtained unexpected numbers of new members, or to Turkey, where, through dubious intermediaries, a membership base was established, which would later send a large group of Turkish transsexuals to the next transnational Congress in Italy.

The project soon came to terms with the economic and organisational constraints of an era without Internet and divided by the Iron Curtain. But the intuition was the right one: an increasingly interdependent world requires a planetary politics capable of acting on the entire continuum of interdependence. This is the second condition placed by Zhao Tingyang for the *Tianxia* system: the *political* dimension, and that means the development of structures capable of governing the world as a premise for governing the country. A transnational party would be a *rhizomatic party*, capable of bringing participation and the voice of citizens to the same height as a world system that surpasses and overwhelms impotent national politics.

The ambition to establish, from scratch, a transnational party with a truly planetary participation must not appear as something unrealistic. It is, in fact, now possible to imagine such a development. Moreover, even before the construction of new political forces on a directly transnational level, what we desperately need today is a *transnationalisation* of already existing structures of political participation, infiltrating a new planetary logic into parties, chancelleries and town halls, unions and movements and into the political life of each one of us.

Imagine, for example, a party that did not limit its membership on the basis of nationality, but actively sought participation from anywhere in the planet, including other organised political forces, trade unions, civil society platforms and social movements wishing to engage in an innovative experiment in global coordination.

Imagine a transnational party running for government in a national context but accepting the contribution of people from other countries in its programme, so as to bring the excluded into the national parliament and subvert the limits of that institution.

This would imply a party able to give the *conventions* that govern the world, and define our lives, all the importance they merit. Trade treaties, for instance, are among the policies that most influence, limit, improve or worsen labour, environmental and welfare standards. Despite this, they are often relegated to the bottom of the political agenda and public debate. Even where a debate is present, this is often limited to challenging the treaties in force or under negotiation, rather than drawing up and advancing, in unison, new agreements from which all the populations involved would benefit. How many of us know what the discussions, wishes and aspirations of Indian or Japanese civil society are during the negotiation of a trade treaty? And above all: how many of the political parties and governments know this or are interested in it? Imagine instead a party that involved individuals and civil society from India in its deliberations on the advantages and disadvantages of such an agreement and that would work out together a proposal capable of raising standards in both continents, around which to mobilise and campaign in all countries touched by the agreement. Trade treaties are one of the most powerful instruments for changing the approach of labour policies and the distribution of wealth. If market access were truly linked, for instance, to the stipulation of appropriate labour, social and ecological standards, it would have the capacity to ensure an upward race for all. We should stop playing defensively, fighting against the trade treaties that are imposed on us in an often opaque and cowardly way, and instead learn to *politicise* the market and go on the offensive, developing ambitious and articulated proposals for new trade agreements. To recognise how far we are from such a situation just think of the utter inability of UK and European progressives to come together and draft, jointly, a blueprint for a new positive relation following Brexit. And the reason for this is precisely the national blind spots in even the most well-meaning of political parties.

Or try asking yourself this question: many national parties talk about governing migration in cooperation with countries of origin and investing in Africa's development, but how many have actually had relations with political forces, trade unions, or representatives of African civil society to think and work together on a shared plan? Imagine a party that brought together its partners from Europe and Africa to develop a common programme for the management of migration flows and for the relationship between the two continents. The seriousness of the proposal would undoubtedly benefit, as would most probably its justice, its effectiveness and its ability to be taken up by both the countries of arrival and those of origin.

Everyone can think of many other examples. The point common to them all is this: in order to recover a real political agency on the deployment of world interdependence we must move from an international relation to a common relationship between world citizens within shared political spaces. Political parties offer a stupendous opportunity for opening up such experimentation.

Planetary parties would also have the benefit of bringing a new understanding of temporality. Their work would take place in the long term: not just organising a platform, protest or addressing short-term national priorities, but developing

97

a continuity of action capable of shaping a transformation of our planetary organisation. Too often social activation appears to follow the dictates of historical development rather than precede them. And this is all the truer with parties, fixated as they are with focus groups that photograph existing reality and forgetful of their original ambition: to shape the conditions for the transformation, and not the mere mirroring, of that same reality.

A planetary party would aim to prefigure and guide the development of a new paradigm. It was precisely a similar obstinacy and confidence in one's own beliefs and ideals that guaranteed neoliberalism its success – from its first theorisation in the 1920s, via its acceptance in the 1970s, to its peak in the 1990s. Hayek admitted this without mincing his words, even going so far as to invoke a new policy of utopia: 'What we lack is a liberal Utopia', he wrote, 'which does not confine itself to what appears today as politically possible.' And, to achieve this, what is needed is '. . . intellectual leaders who are willing to work for an ideal, however small may be the prospects of its early realization'.[1] It is highly telling that while neoliberalism has internalised this high concept of historical transformation, much progressive vision has been reduced to limited short-sightedness.

In 2018, a fifteen-year-old girl, Greta Thunberg, caused a sensation after yet another inconclusive UN climate change conference, releasing an avalanche that would soon bring hundreds of thousands of people to the world's squares. In simple and direct words, she accused the entire world leadership of having abdicated all responsibility for the protection of future generations. Greta imagined herself in 2078, when she would turn seventy-five. She imagined her children celebrating that day with her and asking her why, when the climate disaster could still be stopped, no one acted. Precisely this future projection appears dramatically absent today, despite our technological jump. We continue to destroy the only planet at our disposal while elites worry about immediate profit, the next board of directors or the next election. It is as if we all already inhabited the dystopian world painted by *Children of Men*, the film by director Alfonso Cuarón, where a strange virus suddenly makes humanity sterile. Those left alive are, literally, *the last men*. The temporal dimension is crushed, while the hourglass of humanity sweats its last grains. There is no more human future; only a present that marches towards its final dissolution.

But we are not the last men and the last women. History cannot be put in a box; you cannot give up time and leave the scene. The task before us, strengthened by historical experience and heightened human connection, is to prepare collectively and politically the next round of our *ouroboros*, the next round of organisation of our planet, thus managing to determine the exit from our present moment of crisis without waiting for its resolution in the form of a planetary catastrophe.

This is a task that requires unprecedented ambition and vision and a capacity to act, in concert, beyond borders. This is what political parties ought to be able to provide, surpassing their national limitations and addictions. Developing new planetary parties would mean restoring ambition to change and building the tools for its construction over time. But it is a promise that stretches well beyond party politics.

A planetary people

We know that overcoming the obvious limits of exclusively national climate action means building a global movement capable of changing common sense about the climate crisis. However important the actions that some states may take, we know there is no 'ecologism in one country' today. But there is more. The discussions on the *anthropocene*, the era in which humanity itself shapes the becoming of nature, bring us back to a trivial yet disruptive consideration: humanity-as-such has transformed itself into a historical subject acting on its own environment as a single force. We are already a common political subject – albeit not recognised as such and still with minimal self-awareness – whose common action is exerting a dramatic and destructive transformation of its habitat.

Similar considerations can be made regarding our stance faced with threats of epidemics, as became abundantly clear during the coronavirus crisis in the early 2020s. Distinctions between national polities lose any meaning – containment measures cannot work in a single country, for as long as a virus thrives somewhere it can spread anywhere. In this sense, even the protection of economic supremacy becomes of only relative importance. It is humanity-as-such that faces a common threat, and the threat will either go away for the entirety of humanity or it will remain to haunt every member of it.

We seem to inhabit a new *negative communism*, a community of destiny that manifests itself through the disappearance of a habitable planet, of a just economy, or a healthy environment. We have privatised the profits and socialised the apocalypse.

And yet our reaction is far from united. Quite on the contrary, the trend risks entrenching a rush towards planetary gated communities separating the privileged few from the damned many. Far from acting as a great leveller, the coronavirus crisis showed the extent of the class dynamic of contemporary catastrophes – with low-paid workers exposed to contagion on public transport on their way to work and white-collar employees connecting via conference calls. The climate crisis will only give greater urgency to this process; the concept of 'climate apartheid' is rapidly entering the public debate to signal the great gap that is being created between those who can pay for (however temporary) salvation and those who are forced to face the worst consequences of climate disasters. As biogenetic enhancement becomes an increasingly concrete perspective, we can imagine a near future where *a part* of humanity will succeed, through its wealth and privileged position, to augment its mental and physical skills, leaving the rest behind and transforming the difference between classes into something that borders on the difference between species. This is in some ways a postmodern return to the past: and namely to a time when the difference between rich and poor was clearly identifiable by pronounced differences in life expectancy, appearance and health.

This is a complete betrayal of the third condition of *Tianxia* – taking the entirety of humanity as the endpoint of action. We must resist the new medievalism of class enclosures and restore a positive common interest and a renewed capacity for action around it. This is the round of *ouroboros* of our time: the integration of humanity, made evident by its potential extinction and by its vulnerability vis-à-vis nature, seems to have far exceeded our capacity to understand and govern that interdependence and power. With the same mechanism of historical delay that we have recounted many times, the unity of the world is once again one step ahead of us. This is the constituent value – the ability to constitute the world and build a people – of the climate breakdown. Because in the face of the risk of environmental collapse there is no homeland that is not the whole world and there is no community of destiny that is not humanity as such.

Ideas, suggestions, or traces have all historically exercised an extraordinary power of mobilisation. They have managed, on many occasions, to transform a merely material reality into a collective stance. Just think of the workers' movement: the simple presence of individually exploited workers did not in itself justify the construction of a movement, it did not lead, as a mathematical solution of a materialist equation, to collective consciousness and mobilisation. For this to happen a suggestion was needed: that of class solidarity. One often associated with an eschatological landscape: that of socialism or communism, or at least of the various 'possible worlds'. The conclusion is simple: humans have the ability to tilt on the basis of a proposed revolution in society. And a sufficient number of inclinations turn the prospect of an unreachable utopia into a concrete reality and in the process give birth to a new collective identity.

The ideal inclination that builds a movement also transforms the participants themselves, weaving a new sense of belonging and common interest that in turn becomes an indispensable driver of change. Since its first conception in ancient Greece, the *demos* was thought of as an artificial subjectivity, built through political acts and the creation of institutions, and not as a closed and naturally cohesive community, an *ethnos*. Indeed, all communities, even those that today we call national, have always been contested spaces crossed by conflicts and exclusions; the *territory* has never been naturally and equally *of all* the inhabitants. Just think of Virginia Woolf's famous book title, *A Room of One's Own*. The choice of the spatiality of a room is not accidental: what is denied to women in a patriarchal society is precisely a territory. There is nothing as false as a certain nostalgia that recreates the fiction of a lost organic past that belonged equally to all members of the nation, and over which control must be regained and which must be freed from foreign contamination.

The national people has always been justified and defined *a posteriori* through the construction of modern statehood. And, as has happened in the past, albeit in forms and shapes still unimaginable, a new planetary demos will emerge through the act of thinking and acting collectively around the great challenges that humanity, as a whole, is facing today. Just as the socialist aspiration has built and prefigured a new social subject, transforming a shapeless mass of individual workers into the workers' movement, so the aspiration for a planet that remains habitable for humanity requires the emergence of a new people with a consciousness equal to the necessary planetary transformation.

Parties and people, aware of their planetary destiny and of the vertiginous task of rebuilding a world, form the necessary builders for new planetary institutions.

Planetary institutions

Just as a people is constructed, so are institutions. For too long we have abandoned the ambition to implement far-reaching policies and to transform the world's institutions into an instrument for their implementation and generalisation. This is precisely what parties and movements with a planetary gaze ought to do.

In 2018, something new began to happen: on both sides of the Atlantic, in the United States and in Europe, the demands for a Green New Deal became louder and louder. As the name implies, the reference is to the New Deal programme carried out by American President Franklin D. Roosevelt in the 1930s. The original programme laid its foundations not only in the Great Depression but in an unprecedented climate emergency, the Dust Bowl. Sandstorms, unregulated use of pesticides, and intensive cultivation burned the soil of the Great Plains of the United States, causing misery, migration, and a gigantic agricultural crisis. This is the story told in *The Grapes of Wrath*, John Steinbeck's masterpiece, where the Joads are forced to migrate from Oklahoma to California after the drought. The institutional answer was unprecedented: with the Conservation Civilian Corps, the US government directly employed millions of workers in environmental conservation, planting up to three billion new trees and building dams, bridges and new protected areas. It was a national mobilisation unprecedented in peacetime.

To make the original New Deal concrete, Roosevelt found himself leading a strengthening and expansion of the role of the federal state, giving it new powers of action and a significantly increased budget. Well before a transformation of economic policy, the New Deal brought with it a transformation of the role and powers of the public administration of the United States. Today's Green plans can acquire a similar constituent value. Deploying the necessary financial, economic and management capacity to transform complex and heterogeneous economic spaces requires a new capacity for transnational action and therefore a new institutionality.

Think of the European Union. The European project was born from the perspective of the political unity of the continent through gradual economic integration. This functionalist logic has failed. Those who expected that the euro, a common currency without a government and a monetary union without a fiscal union, could surreptitiously force the constitution of that very government and that missing fiscal union are now faced with the risk of the opposite result. Integration through currency has resulted in harmful economic policies that have alienated, and not brought closer, the peoples of Europe. Perhaps the need to transform our development model now offers an unprecedented opportunity: completing the European construction through an impressive and ambitious programme of ecological transformation.

The same is true of global institutions. Think of the basic structures of so-called world governance: from the International Monetary Fund to the World Bank. As we have seen, most of these organs formed with Bretton Woods and were hijacked with the emergence of neoliberal globalisation. Their role is significant: every Argentinean or Greek citizen has recent experience of what 'IMF' means. But why does our politics so rarely – in fact, never – put their reform at the centre of political initiatives? Yet these are institutions that, if renewed, could represent a kernel of today's much-needed transformation of the world. The World Bank, for instance, could help by flooding our societies with liquidity to ensure the ecological and energy transformation that is essential to save humanity from the worst effects of the climate crisis. And the International Monetary Fund, also thanks to the new digital revolution, could bring back its original aspiration: promoting a genuine world currency to stem and reduce the destructive power of capital flows. Why would we let a private company such as Facebook try its hand at establishing a planetary currency, and not try letting collective decisions and political processes guide such an attempt?

Or think of the World Health Organisation. The coronavirus epidemic that spread across the planet at the beginning of 2020 has demonstrated the dramatic interdependence reached by the world system. Not only do viruses cross all borders: the diverging health and welfare standards across countries represent a threat to all of us. A planetary investment in decent healthcare and hygienic standards is no longer a matter of charity or solidarity: it is a matter of self-interest. The World Health Organisation is at the moment unable even to guarantee access to 460 life-saving medicines, which it declared, over forty years ago, should be accessible to all. The time may have arrived to argue for its transformation into a true planetary institution able to intervene, and fund, investment in health services across our planet, addressing the threat posed *to all of us* of millions still living without any access to healthcare and billions living in communities that are unable to provide adequate health support.

Or, finally, think of institutions that are perhaps less well known but potentially key, such as the International Labour Organisation, whose slogan sounds like a hymn to interdependence: 'Poverty anywhere is a danger to prosperity everywhere.' Even though it is one of the oldest international institutions – it was founded in 1919, at the end of the First World War and together with the system of the League of Nations – and although it deals with one of the most important and heartfelt issues today, over the years the organisation has gradually lost all radicality and has seen its relevance wane. This withering away has taken place at a time when the global attack on labour would make the ILO more necessary than ever. But does it have to be this way? Not at all. In fact, it is precisely new labour policies already applicable at national level *but with planetary impacts* that may represent an important line of attack against the diminishing dignity of labour and social rights everywhere.

Workers of the world . . .

If neoliberal globalisation is based on a dense network of international agreements that govern financial flows and trade practices and structure the 'golden straitjacket' of states, then what we need are *new agreements*, constructed politically and capable of providing a positive and democratic planetary constraint. This is perhaps the most pertinent element for what a new world system should guarantee: the possibility that any regulation, agreement or new policy or institution will lead to a generalised improvement in planetary living conditions for humanity as a whole. This is the third, at once social and moral, characteristic of *Tianxia*.

Among the most successful tools in weakening, disciplining and exploiting labour is the international logic applied to competition between workers. In a perverse game of mirrors, the reduction in labour protection in Western countries is increasingly blamed on competition from emerging countries. This is a tendency that creates proselytes even among some progressive forces. The attack on unfair competition from China, for example, is common rhetoric even in some of the best-known figures of American progressivism. Just as competition from Eastern European countries is being targeted by Western European nationalisms, including at times on the left.

This forms the basis of the argument that workers and the middle classes in emerging countries have relatively benefited from globalisation, while those in advanced countries have suffered its effects. But are there really conflicting interests between the two groups? Yes, there are, *but only if we accept competition between workers as a premise and a fact*. What if we were to consider this situation not as a natural given but as a contingent political reality and conceived *all workers* as losers within this system? Then downward competition, regardless of how the crumbs are distributed and regardless of the relative increase or stagnation of low salaries, would be seen to cut *a vast majority* of humanity out of the enormous wealth accumulated by a very small oligarchic class.

Too often, any difference between multinationals, workers and governments is made to collapse, failing to differentiate competition between nations from the dynamics of conflict between workers and employers *in whatever country each of them may be based*. Instead of exploring and getting involved in a productive system that generates extraordinary subjectivity and conflict, we accept the representation of this complexity in terms of a competition between nations, with the organic interests of one people opposed to those of another. It is as if we had become incapable of conceiving workers from third countries as subjects of conflict and not as extras in a trade war between states. But if we look at the most important protests by Chinese workers, for instance, we soon discover that they are often directed towards Western multinationals, including well-known names such as Amazon or the leader of American retail, Walmart. We find ourselves in this paradoxical situation: Chinese workers are fighting against an American giant to improve their wage conditions, while the United States does not lift a finger to regulate its transnational companies but instead accuses China of unfair competition based precisely on low labour costs. We can do better.

A little-known ancient American law – the Alien Tort Claims Act, passed in 1789 – allows citizens from all over the world access to US courts of justice if they have been the victim of a violation of international law or of a US treaty. It is an extraordinary cosmopolitan innovation for the law of the time, anticipating by a few years Immanuel Kant's 1795 *Perpetual Peace: A Philosophical Sketch*, a text often seen as the inaugural gesture of modern legal cosmopolitanism. The law remained virtually unused until 1980, when an American court decided to accept an appeal by a Paraguayan citizen against a compatriot living in the United States and accused of torturing him. Since then, albeit in a highly uncertain legal environment, the instrument has started to be used against both individuals and multinational corporations. The lawsuit brought by Chinese journalists Wang Xiaoning and Shi Tao, who accused Yahoo of allowing the Chinese government to access their e-mail accounts, causing their arrest and torture, made headlines. The American courts decided to accept the case on the very basis of the Alien Tort Claims Act, which prompted Yahoo to acknowledge its responsibilities and negotiate an agreement between the parties.

As is normal for a law written more than two centuries ago, its application remains contested and the judgments of the courts are often contradictory. But it would not be difficult to imagine a modern drafting of such legislation, so that all those multinationals accused of promoting unfair labour practices, such as the repression of trade unions, child labour, unpaid overtime and so on, or practices harmful to the environment, as common in low-cost garment production, could be brought to court. Workers and citizens around the world could sue multinational companies for unpaid wages, trade union repression, or pollution *using the courts and standards of the countries of origin of the multinational.* A simple legal innovation of this kind would allow workers, perhaps helped by planetary parties, NGOs and trade unions, to make their voices heard and to put under the spotlight all those practices that lie at the root of the great exploitation of global labour and downward competition. And the most interesting aspect? All it would take is a *local* legislative change, limited to one or more jurisdictions, to achieve a transformation in the political strength of workers in *every part of the world.*

This would not be a simple moral imperative to comply with the third condition of *Tianxia*, but self-interest. Planetary interdependence means there are very few policies capable of benefiting the entire population of one country at the expense of another; instead, we face transversal and transnational interests that put *one part of the world,* for example that which depends on labour to survive, against another part, for example that which depends on rent. This is not about guaranteeing a concept, however sacrosanct, of global justice between countries; but rather to reverse social dumping and favour workers in poor and rich countries alike, by rebalancing the gap between salaries and profits. Ultimately, this is about guaranteeing individual workers the same rights of cosmopolitan citizenship that multinational corporations already enjoy almost exclusively.

Such a development would also have the merit of providing trade unions with a clear and simple perimeter of action: working side by side with unions in poorer countries to map such abuses and bring the most important cases before the courts of the multinationals' home countries. It is something that would call forward a greater planetary engagement of labour forces, at a time when unions appear to have mostly subcontracted the protest against the conditions of global exploitation to global justice activists. Far gone are the days of the Industrial Workers of the World Union, the Wobblies, founded in Chicago in 1905 explicitly as a world union with the ambition to open offices in dozens of countries. But this is precisely the spirit that now needs to be recuperated.

An oracle for the world

How much does a kilogram weigh? Far from being tautological, the question has engaged scientists for years. Still to this day the prototype of the kilogram is kept under a triple glass case in a vault in Paris. Despite the best intentions, however, its mass tends to vary, as some microparticles of pollution still manage to creep in, causing an oscillation, however infinitesimal, of its weight – so as to make the kilogram actually heavier than a kilogram. The archaic nature of measurement should come as no surprise; suffice it to say that the exact measurement of the metre is carved in stone in a wall of the Parthenon in Paris.

It is no coincidence that the *ville lumière* is always involved: it is precisely the rationalist approach of the French Revolution that generalised the new system of decimal measurements. Together with the transition from the axe to the more aseptic guillotine, the cacophony of measures of the *ancien régime* was abandoned in favour of a more logical system; no more kings' feet and vassals' thumbs. The universalisation of weights and lengths led to a new global standard that became the heritage of all humanity; the possibility of weighing and measuring rationally was acquired and spread throughout the planet – with some irrational exceptions in the Anglo-Saxon world – as already happened previously for Arabic numerals or the principle of an elementary alphabet. This was nothing less than a 'common good' of humanity: it would be ridiculous if you had to pay a copyright to the inventor of the metric system every time you put up a shelf in the house. And yet, this is precisely what happens when you do a search on the Internet.

We know that Google's economic model is based on a near-exclusive monopoly of our search data and the sale of targeted advertisements through that information. But what if Google was such a disruptive company and its founders such brilliant minds as to have invented a new *planetary human right*?

Access to information has become the centre-piece of the new global economy; never before has knowledge truly been power to such an extent. And it is precisely information and com-munication technologies that make it possible to produce and access this knowledge. But it is clear that it is the choice of *which* information to make available first, and at what price, that makes all the difference. We relate to Google as a magic box that answers all our questions. But do we really want a private oracle? What if we took up the universalist aspirations of the French Revolution and built a new planetary right to search the world's information and connect with the world's citizens *free of economic and political interference*?

Yes, the first condition disrupts the business model of many digital corporations, and the second the business model of many authoritarian regimes. And this is precisely what we need. Algorithms are increasingly the yardstick by which common sense is measured: what is acceptable and what lies outside the chorus. The novelty represented by the manipulation of big data is the possibility of a voluntary control; that is, the possibility of directing our own desires while making it appear as a natural and autonomous choice. This is an extraordinary power over our consciences that is currently the domain of two powers alone: Silicon Valley with the NSA and the Chinese Communist Party.

Just think how different the programming of algorithms is in the West or China. The market algorithm, the one at the base of systems like YouTube or Facebook, tends to favour the most extreme and divisive messages. The entire fake news industry is based on this very concept: the more scandalous the message, the more it will capture attention and therefore the higher will it be pushed by the algorithms. Recent studies have shown that YouTube's algorithm, with the same principle, tends to suggest slightly more extreme videos than the ones we just watched, so as to keep our attention for longer. The Chinese algorithm, on the other hand, takes a completely different direction. Instead of suggesting stronger and therefore more polarising and divisive content, it suggests information in line with central government directives. In a context where political stability is more important than short-term profit, digital manipulation favours convergence towards homogeneity, in continuity with the directives issued in 2018 by Xi Jinping for an Internet capable of 'spreading positive information, maintaining the right political direction and guiding public opinion and values in the right direction'.

The same dynamic applies to data and their power to predict future actions. It is a concept with which we are all familiar: the data released by our web browsing allow an analysis of our needs at a given time and therefore inform the type of advertising we will see. In China, this mechanism is increasingly being used to isolate potentially deviant traits – as is already happening in the Muslim province of Xinjiang. But the market system can rely on the same operation: increasing health insurance premiums in the US, for example, on the basis of spying on our current behaviour.

The scandalous truth is this: one of the most important transformations in our way of decoding, understanding and judging the world is being left either to the profit logic of a handful of large private American companies or to the political control of a giant authoritarian party.

It is quite possible to imagine the administration of a universal search system as a *global common*. Allowing us all, therefore, to decide and not suffer the choice of use for the data thus collected. We are all acquainted with the concept of a public company or nationalised enterprise. Some of the most complex operations are run in this way, such as managing rail traffic in almost all advanced countries or running the power grid. But public management stops at national borders. Leaving everything that surpasses them at the mercy of market dynamics or old international diplomacy.

Why should it be seen as impossible not to *nationalise* but *internationalise* Google's search algorithm? Why not imagine a new planetary institution capable of managing a global common good in the interest of all humanity, enabling a diffused system to emerge and thrive anchored on a common use of data as a shared global commons?

This must not necessarily take the form of an ambitious and yet potentially impossible expropriation. The desire of freeing data from the totalitarian control of private companies or authoritarian states can take many shapes and forms, including different elements of regulations enabling a more plural ecosystem to emerge – such as imagined by artist Jonas Staal and lawyer Jan Fermon with their project Collectivise Facebook, advancing a collective action lawsuit to force legal recognition of Facebook as a public domain that should be under ownership and control of its users.

Wishful thinking as it may sound, we must be

able to recuperate radicality and ambition in our desires and demands, as Hayek warned us. Our planetary lenses allow us to do just that. We have an enemy to help us achieve that.

A planetary class enemy

Modern European nations were established by taking away the power of taxation from the aristocratic potentate and the feudal regime, thus centralising the accumulation and use of economic resources in a new unitary taxation system, which in turn enabled the institution of a national standing army, a national bureaucracy, and all the traits that we now associate with modern centralised statehood. It should therefore come as no surprise that the destructuring of national sovereignty in our day goes hand-in-hand with a national fiscal crisis.

We know just how much neoliberal globalisation depends on the system of tax havens and on the ability of organised wealth to play state against state in a game of fiscal competition. The race to the bottom is not limited to labour rights, but it involves modern state constructions in their entirety, with particular emphasis on fiscal justice and the distribution of wealth. It is a well-documented process that leads to absolutely unsustainable situations: companies such as Google that are subject to a fraction of the taxes levied at an employee or a professional; companies such as Apple that store in tax havens financial reserves that far exceed the availability of foreign currency of any European country. It is this same process, which goes well beyond a handful of well-known large multinationals and embraces major parts of the system of wealth creation, that also leads to the disconnection of transnational elites from their national communities. Taking up the 'two worlds' that we have previously presented, we see how fiscal capacity, and therefore redistributive justice, is limited in the narrow spaces of *imperium* and national statehood, while capital, and its incessant accumulation, travels freely in the global space of the *dominium* of money. A division of this kind builds *de facto* two transnational fiscal and hence social classes: those who inhabit the world of politics, with its suffocating taxes and public budgets in crisis, and those who flap their wings over every fiscal frontier.

There are many and very elaborate proposals

on how to address such scandal, at both regional and planetary level. A common European tax on large assets and a common tax on the profits of multinationals, for instance, would have the possibility of building a new, broad-based taxation from scratch, recovering resources that are currently unattainable for national jurisdictions. Not to mention the possibility of building a world tax authority working to prevent a tiny class of multi-billionaires from extorting immeasurable profits and taking them away from the tax authorities of every country. We are talking about a stratospheric figure: there are more than 8,000 billion dollars parked in tax havens, equivalent to an exorbitant ten per cent of world wealth. Think, for example, of a minimum global taxation on business profits and a global taxation on wealth, instruments capable of closing any space for scandalous tax avoidance and directing the extraordinary revenue thus acquired to projects of global ecological transformation, opening the doors to a Global Green New Deal.

If there is a lack of serious mechanisms at national level to tax the concentration of wealth fairly, and no ability to do so beyond the state, then it follows that states compete for the crumbs. But if the international system tolerates and makes organised robbery possible, we cannot content ourselves with fighting for what is left in the till. It is no exaggeration to say that the battle on fiscal justice is the main step towards the establishment of a planetary politics worthy of the name.

This provides one much-needed element of politics: an enemy. The organised system of tax dodging, replete with its billionaires and multinationals, is nothing short of a twenty-first-century version of a class enemy. Indeed, their wealth and power is premised precisely on maintaining a clear inadequacy on the three conditions we have seen to be at the basis of *Tianxia*: there needs to be a common economic planetary space, deprived, however, of any political dimension and without any inclination in taking the benefit of humanity as a whole as its endpoint.

It is worth remembering that the very demand for fiscal justice has been the basis of more general and often revolutionary political claims. On 20 June 1789 in France the representatives of the Third State abandoned the General States, called themselves the National Assembly, and swore not to separate until the Constitution was established. The Tennis Court Oath, so named for the field on which it took place, marked a decisive change in the political dynamics of the French Revolution. The demand would no longer be for better policies and fairer taxation, but for a transformation in the system of government, considered incapable of responding to the needs of citizenship and structurally linked to the interests of the privileged classes. The result was revolution and the birth of modern nation states. The world today needs its own Tennis Court Oath, its own planetary revolution and the birth of its own planetary politics.

意味

We began this book by telling the story of the colony of the world, of the process that has led all our countries to a condition of extraordinary provincialisation in the face of the global challenges that grow around us. We have argued that it is precisely this gap; that is, the reluctance of current political systems to operate beyond the limits and constraints provided by the international regime, that feeds our democratic crisis and our inability to transform political struggle into real change.

The refusal to overcome the material and mental limits of the nation does not only affect our political agency but reduces the depth of our field of vision towards the future, reducing our thinking to the merely attainable and the ordinary. A new planetary politics offers us the possibility of abandoning a politics that has become a mere technical adjustment of the market algorithm and of going back to imagining the radically otherwise and of turning our actions into the metaphor of the world to come. Taking back the world means taking back utopia.

We have the privilege and the curse to be alive at a historical time in which the categories of modernity, and first and foremost that of the nation state, melt before our eyes. This is a moment of uncertainty, insecurity and anger. But it is also a time of extraordinary opportunity. It is a moment fit for what Immanuel Wallerstein termed 'utopistics',[1] arguing that in a time of systemic bifurcation – what we have termed a round of *ouroboros* – stable systems become chaotic. These are moments when it becomes possible to reconstruct a new horizon of meaning with an ambition and scale previously unimaginable. A real planetary turn will require time, work and resources. The ideas presented here are nothing but notes in the margin on the direction to take. A trace, contradictory and incomplete. But this is the time of possibility.

意味

We narrated a story that began with Stefan Zweig in 1914 and ends today. All this time encompasses but one lifetime. 1914 was also the date of my grandfather's birth. He died at 104. To look at the historical transformations that his life has witnessed throws into ridicule any attempt to make us believe that it is today impossible to transform our countries and reclaim our planet. History never ends. And history is never written. But it is defined by men and women through action, desire, ambition, hope and will. Imagine an Italian citizen, abducted by aliens in 1935, and brought back to Rome only twenty years later. She would have left a continent prey to Nazism and Fascism, a world in which Italian gases stifled the Ethiopian people, a world in which the poor were left to die of curable diseases and in which the vast majority of the country lived in an impoverished countryside. And she would return to a democratic republic, to a world in decolonisation that saw the decline of empires, to a country that sanctioned and guaranteed the universal right to health and in which a new industrialisation was transforming, as Pasolini so well narrated, the peasant masses into the new urban and consumerist petty bourgeoisie. Twenty years of furious acceleration – and how little is two decades? – that have changed our world. In between, lay the tragedy of the Second World War. Time has not stopped today. On the contrary, it is accelerating. And the dizzying historical task of our generation is to govern this acceleration, without once again letting a catastrophe determine its outcome.

The Chinese concept of *Yi-Wei* (意味) combines the character of *meaning* and the character of *taste*. It indicates an idea that shows itself not with the lucidity and clarity of logical thought but with the progressive unfolding of a taste in the mouth. A meaning that envelops the tongue and slowly allows itself to be intuited; a sense that cannot be defined in a static way but that evolves, disappears and returns. If there is a taste, and a meaning, that I hope this book will leave, then it is that of possibility, of hope and of ambition. We no longer understand the world. And that is just fine. We have collectively achieved what philosophy calls a state of *aporia*. And, as Socrates teaches us, this is precisely the place to start to rebuild a new meaning and a new world.

Notes

The twilight of universal Europe

1 Stefan Zweig, *Messages from a Lost World: Europe on the Brink* (London: Pushkin Press, 2016).

2 Pankaj Mishra, *Age of Anger: A History of the Present* (London: Allen Lane, 2017).

3 Karl Polanyi, *The Great Transformation* (Boston: Beacon Press, 2001).

4 Hannah Arendt, *The Origins of Totalitarism* (London: Penguin, 2017).

5 Leon Trotsky, 'Is the Slogan "The United States of Europe" a Timely One?': http://www.marxists.org/archive/trotsky/1924/ ffyci-2/25b.htm.

6 Antonio Gramsci, *Quaderni del carcere* (Torino: Einaudi, 1975): *Quaderno 15*. Translation by the author.

The human zoo

1 David Goodhart, *The Road to Somewhere: The Populist Revolt and the Future of Politics* (London: Hurst, 2017).

2 Jennifer Bair, 'Taking Aim at the New International Economic Order', in Philip Mirowski and Dieter Plehwe (eds), *The Road from Mont Pèlerin* (Cambridge, MA: Harvard University Press, 2009).

3 For all its global ambitions, Bretton Woods was a fragile system and one heavily dependent on the United States. If the economist John Maynard Keynes, representing Great Britain, advocated the need for a new world currency, his former disciple Harry Dexter White, representing the United States, argued that such a global currency should be the dollar. And so it will come to be, giving the American currency the status of world reserve that still today allows the United States to contravene the most trivial budgetary rules and exercise overwhelming financial discretionality. Yet, by siding with partisan financial interests, the Bretton Woods system became dependent on the ability of the United States to maintain a balanced financial position with the rest of the world, making an imbalance in the United States the source of immediate tensions on the entire world system. It is precisely this coupling, this national partiality of the new world system, that would eventually decree its crisis.

The last ideology

1 Quinn Slobodian, *Globalists: The End of Empire and the Birth of Neoliberalism* (Cambridge, MA: Harvard University Press, 2018), Kindle locations 4402–8.
2 Milton Friedman, *The Lexus and the Olive Tree* (London: Picador, 2012), p. 109.

Before the revolution

1 Simone Weil, *Oppression and Liberty* (Chicago: University of Massachusetts Press, 1978), p. 10.
2 Douglas Rushkoff, 'Survival of the Richest, "Medium"', 5 July 2018: https://medium.com/s/futurehuman/survival-of-the-richest-9ef6cdddocci.
3 Wendy Brown, *Walled States, Waning Sovereignty* (New York: Zone Books, 2017), Kindle location 90.
4 Richard Rorty, 'Unger, Castoriadis, and the Romance of a National Future': http://www.robertounger.com/en/wp-content/uploads/2017/10/discussions2.pdf.

All under heaven

1 Zhao Tingyang, *Tianxia: tout sous un même ciel* (Paris: Les Éditions du Cerf, 2018), p. 275. Translation by the author.
2 Ibid., p. 272.
3 Wilhelm Röpke, *Economic Order and International Law* (Leiden: A. W. Sijthoff, 1955), p. 250. Quoted in Quinn Slobodian, *Globalists*, Kindle locations 5929–30.

4 Antonio Gramsci, *Quaderni dal carcere: Quaderno 6*, pp. 690–1.
5 Ibid., *Quaderno 9*, p. 1988.

A glimpse into a politics for the planet

1 Friedrich Hayek, *Studies in Philosophy, Politics and Economics* (London: Routledge, 1967), pp. 178–94.

意味

1 Immanuel Wallerstein, *Utopistics, or Historical Choices of the Twenty-First Century* (New York: New Press, 1998).